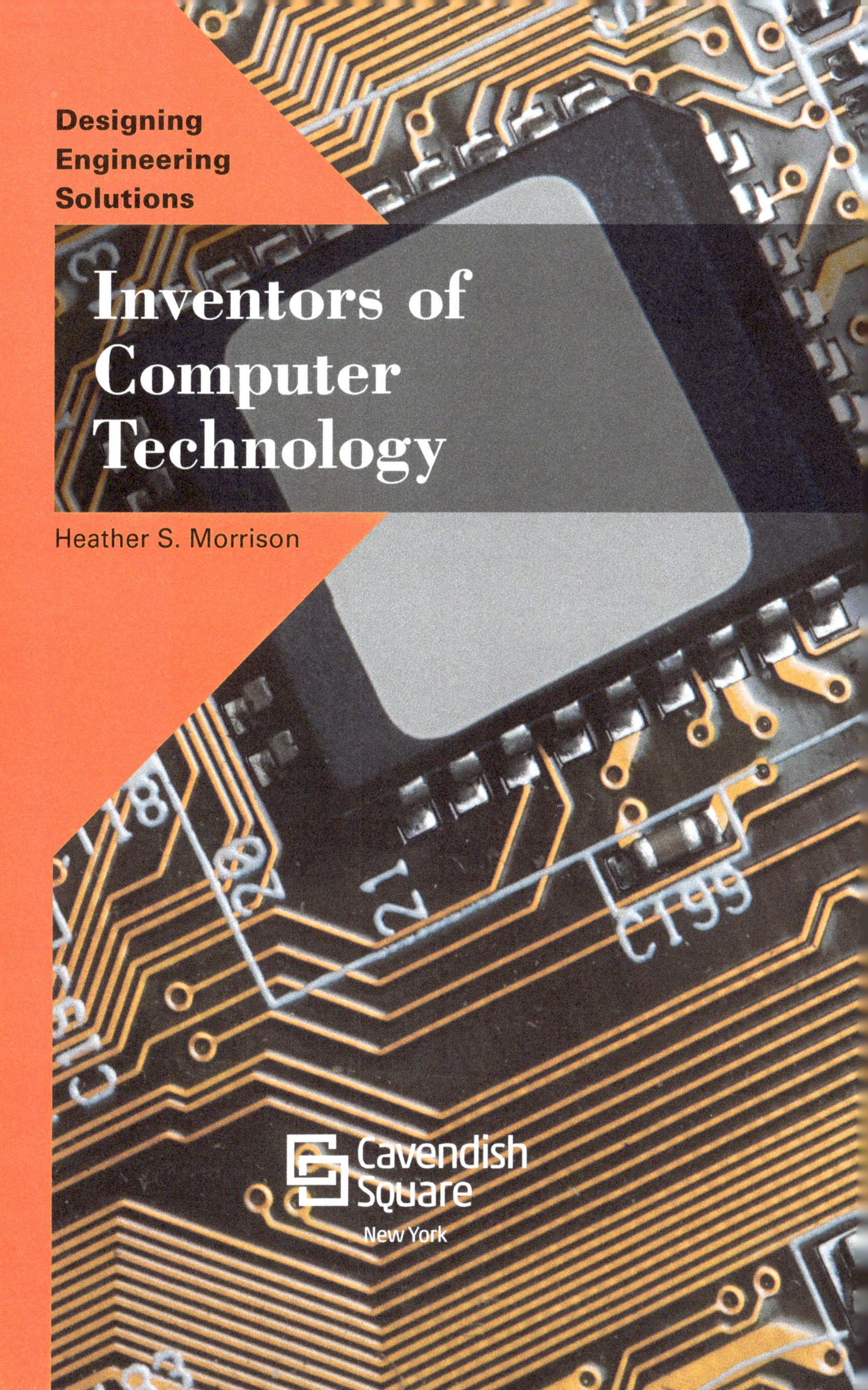
Designing
Engineering
Solutions
Inventors of Computer Technology
Heather S. Morrison
Cavendish Square
New York

Published in 2016 by Cavendish Square Publishing, LLC
243 5th Avenue, Suite 136, New York, NY 10016

First Edition

Website: cavendishsq.com

CPSIA Compliance Information: Batch #WS15CSQ

All websites were available and accurate when this book was sent to press.

Library of Congress Cataloging-in-Publication Data

Morrison, Heather S.
Inventors of computer technology / by Heather S. Morrison.
p. cm. — (Designing engineering solutions)
Includes index.
ISBN 978-1-50260-654-9 (hardcover) ISBN 978-1-50260-655-6 (ebook)
1. Computer scientists Biography Juvenile literature. 2. Computer engineers — Biography — Juvenile literature.
3. Computers — History — Juvenile literature. I. Morrison, Heather S. II. Title.
QA76.17 E53 2016
004.092'2—d23

The author would like to thank the following contributors: Kezia Endsley, Cathleen Small, Mary Sisson, Chris Woodford

Editorial Director: David McNamara
Editor: Kristen Susienka
Copy Editor: Cynthia Roby and Michele Suchomel-Casey
Art Director: Jeffrey Talbot
Designer: Alan Sliwinski
Senior Production Manager: Jennifer Ryder-Talbot
Production Editor: Renni Johnson
Photo Research: J8 Media

The photographs in this book are used by permission and through the courtesy of: Jevgenija Pigozne/Getty Images, cover; iStockphoto.com/FrancescoCorticchia, 4; Giovanni Dall'Orto/File:0142 - Archaeological Museum, Athens - Antikythera mechanism - Photo by Giovanni Dall'Orto, Nov 11 2009.jpg/Wikimedia Commons, 5; Science & Society Picture Library/SSPL/Getty Images, 9; Science Museum London/File:Babbages Difference Engine No 1, 1824-1832. (9660573845).jpg/Wikimedia Commons, 15; File:Charles Babbage - 1860.jpg/Wikimedia Commons, 17; Public Domain/File:Black Box Cockpit Voice Recorder, Model AV557D, Sunderstrand Data Control, Inc., c. 1990s - National Electronics Museum - DSC00090.JPG/Wikimedia Commons, 20; Public Domain/File:WorldWideWeb.png/Wikimedia Commons, 23; Brad Barket/Getty Images, 26; Lewis Whyld/AP Photo; 30; Nicholas Kamm/AFP/Getty Images, 32; Emmanuel Dunand/AFP/Getty Images, 35; Martyn Landi/PA Wire/AP Images, 38; SSPL/Getty Images, 40; Public Domain/File:William S. Burroughs (1855-1898).jpg/Wikimedia Commons, 42; Rusty Kennedy/AP Photo, 45; wwwebmeister/Shutterstock.com, 47; Michael Rhodes, 48; Vm/Getty Images, 52; AGPhotos/Shutterstock.com, 54; John Storey/The LIFE Images Collection/Getty Images, 56; The White House, 59; Sam Yeh/AFP/Getty Images, 61; Daniel Acker/Bloomberg/Getty Images, 62; Susan Biddle/For The Washington Post/Getty Images, 67; iStockphoto.com/Tigermad, 69; AP Photo, 70; Public Domain/MC3 Dustin W. Sisco/File:The guided missile destroyer USS Hopper (DDG 70) leaves Joint Base Pearl Harbor-Hickam, Hawaii, March 18, 2013, for a scheduled deployment 130318-N-XD424-012.jpg/Wikimedia Commons, 73; Rama & Musée Bolo/File:Apple II-IMG 7064.jpg/Wikimedia Commons, 75; DB Apple/picturealliance/dpa/Newscom, 76; Shaun Curry/AFP/Getty Images, 81; Public Domain/File:Eniac.jpg/Wikimedia Commons, 83; I. Inoue/AP Photo, Dan McCoy/Getty Images, 84; Pedrosala/Shutterstock.com, 88–89; iStockphoto.com/zmeel, 94; Graham Hughes/The Canadian Press/AP Photo, 95; NetPhotos/Alamy, 98; Paolo Bona/Shutterstock.com, 101; Brian Harkin/Getty Images, 102; Bill Dally/Shutterstock.com, 105; Dimedrol68/Shutterstock.com, 107; Stephanie Cartier/NWS&T Autumn 2005 (www.nwst.org), 108; Netflix/File:Netflix logo.svg/Wikimedia Commons; 112; John Coulter/Getty Images, 114; Jarno Mela/AFP/Getty Images, 115; Krd/File:LinuxCon Europe Linus Torvalds 04.jpg/Wikimedia Commons, 118; Wikimedia Foundation/File:Wikipedia-logo-v2-en.svg/Wikimedia Commons, 120; Simon Dawson/Bloomberg/Getty Images, 121; Simon Dawson/Bloomberg/Getty Images, 123; 1000 Words/Shutterstock.com, 127; David Paul Morris/Bloomberg/Getty Images, 128; Allyson Magda/Polaris/Newscom, 132.

Printed in the United States of America

Contents

Introduction to Computer Technology

Computers have been around for centuries and have been continuously developing. In their earliest forms, computers were wood-and-metal calculators used for mathematics and science. By the mid-twentieth century, they had become giant electronic machines that occupied entire rooms. Today, many "computers" are not even recognizable as computers: they are the invisible "brains" built into such electronic devices as smartphones, digital music players, tablets, and televisions.

The First Calculators and Computers

Calculators and computers developed early in ancient history. The first calculator, the abacus—developed in Babylonia (now the southeastern part of Iraq) around 500 BCE—remained in use for more than two thousand years. Still popular in China, it consists of beads (representing numbers) that slide along wires, enabling people to carry out complex calculations both quickly and efficiently. The earliest known computer, the Antikythera mechanism, was discovered in 1900 aboard a Roman shipwreck off the coast of Greece. A clock-like device with more than thirty bronze gears, it was housed in a wooden frame decorated with around two thousand characters. It was created as early as the first century BCE and used to calculate the movement of planets and stars.

The Antikythera mechanism is one of the world's earliest computing devices.

As centuries progressed, different people challenged the supremacy of these ancient technologies. In 1642, French mathematician and philosopher Blaise Pascal (1623–1662) made a mechanical calculator, called the Pascaline. It had a series of gears to represent the units—tens, hundreds, and so on—of a decimal number. The gears interlocked and added or subtracted numbers as they rotated.

Several decades later, in the 1670s, German mathematician Gottfried Leibniz (1646–1716) invented a more advanced calculator. Also using gears, it worked in a way broadly similar to Pascal's machine, but it could also multiply, divide, and calculate square roots. Leibniz's calculator pioneered another important feature of modern computers: a temporary memory (register) for storing numbers during a calculation.

Another of Leibniz's significant inventions was a way of representing any decimal number using only the digits zero and one. For example, the decimal number 86 can be represented in binary as 1010110. More than two hundred years later, this simple idea would become the basis of how all computers stored information.

Evolving Technologies

Electronics, a way of controlling machines using electricity, was invented at the beginning of the twentieth century; earlier calculators and computers were entirely mechanical (made from wheels, gears, levers, and so on). Calculators and computers differ in the amount of human direction they need to operate. Whereas a calculator merely carries out actions one by one at the direction of an individual, a computer can perform a sequence of operations with little or no human intervention. The series of instructions a computer follows is called a program.

Calculators began to evolve into computers during the early decades of the nineteenth century. To function as a computer, a calculator needed a mechanism that could store and carry out its programs. Such a device was invented in 1801 by Frenchman Joseph-Marie Jacquard (1752–1834) for controlling a loom. Jacquard's loom was "programmed" using little pieces of card punched with holes. The position of the holes indicated how complex patterns were to be woven in rugs and other textiles.

A modern smartphone contains more powerful computer technology than the giant ENIAC machine dating from 1946. A typical tablet contains faster computer chips than IBM's original 1981 personal computer.

Jacquard's loom inspired British mathematician Charles Babbage (1791–1871), who dreamed of constructing elaborate mechanical computers. Babbage's machines proved too expensive to build and none were completed during his lifetime. Nevertheless, he was the first person to discern how a programmable computer could work. Like all modern computers, his designs had an input (a punched card mechanism, for feeding in numbers), a processor (a complex array of more than fifty thousand gear wheels that did mathematical calculations), and an output (a printing mechanism for showing the results).

Among the first to make practical calculating machines, like the ones Babbage had envisaged, were American inventor William Seward Burroughs (1857–1898) and statistician Herman Hollerith (1860–1929). After developing a simple mechanical calculator, Burroughs formed a company that soon became the biggest manufacturer of adding machines in the United States. The company later moved into making general office machines, such as typewriters and computers. Herman Hollerith's work led in a similar direction. While compiling **data** for the US Census in 1880, he realized he could make a machine that would do the job for him. He later founded the company that in 1924 was renamed International Business Machines (IBM), a pioneer in the computer industry during the twentieth century.

Analog Computers

In the 1920s, Vannevar Bush (1890–1974), a US government scientist, began building complex mechanical calculators known as analog computers. These unwieldy contraptions used rotating shafts, gears, belts, and levers to store numbers and carry out complex calculations. One of them, Bush's Differential Analyzer, was effectively a gigantic abacus, the size of a large room. It was used mainly for military calculations, including those needed to aim artillery shells.

Analog computers led to the creation of digital machines, in which numbers were stored electrically in binary form—the pattern of zeros and ones invented by Leibniz. A prototype binary computer was developed in 1939 by US physicist John Atanasoff (1903–1995) and electrical engineer Clifford Berry (1918–1963). The first major digital computer—one that stored numbers electrically instead of representing them with wheels and belts—was the Harvard Mark I. It was completed at Harvard University in 1946 by mathematician Howard Aiken (1900–1973) and used 3,304 relays, or telephone switches, for storing and calculating numbers. Two years later, scientists at the University of Pennsylvania built ENIAC, the world's first fully electronic computer. Instead of relays, it used almost eighteen thousand vacuum tubes, also known as valves, which operated more quickly. According to its operating manual, "The speed of the ENIAC is at least five hundred times as great as that of any other existing computing machine."

Switching the Scene

Switches, or devices that can be either "on" or "off," can be considered the brain cells of a computer; each one can represent a single binary—zero or one. The more switches a computer has, the more numbers it can store; the faster the switches flick on or off, the faster the computer operates. Vacuum tubes were faster switches than relays, but each one was the size and shape of an adult's thumb; eighteen thousand of them

ENIAC

The modern computer age began in 1946 when John Mauchly (1907–1980) and J. Presper Eckert (1919–1995) of the University of Pennsylvania built a monstrous computer named the ENIAC (Electronic Numerical Integrator and Calculator). The ENIAC was an astonishing feat of engineering, the electronic equivalent of the invention of steamships or the construction of the Brooklyn Bridge. It was approximately 100 feet (30.5 meters) long (the same as five cars parked fender to fender), 8 feet (2.4 m) high, and weighed around 30 tons (27.2 metric tons, as much as five elephants). It had to be that big because it contained 17,468 vacuum tube switches, enough electrical cable to stretch from New York City to Detroit, and around five million hand-soldered electrical connections.

Despite its gargantuan dimensions, the ENIAC was roughly one million times slower than a fast modern PC and a thousand times more expensive. Harry Reed, one of the computer scientists who worked with the ENIAC, described it as "a very personal computer. Now we think of a personal computer as one that you carry around with you. The ENIAC was one that you kind of lived inside." The ENIAC was also much harder to use than a modern PC. It is often described as the world's first fully electronic, general-purpose computer because in theory it could be programmed to do different jobs. In the ENIAC, programming required rewiring the entire machine to work a different way. That was an immensely complex and laborious process and, according to Harry Reed, all part of the challenge: "One was supposed to suffer to do it."

took up a huge amount of space. To work properly, vacuum tubes had to be permanently heated to a high temperature, so they consumed enormous amounts of electricity. Computers were evolving quickly during the 1940s, largely driven by military needs. Yet the size, weight, and power consumption of vacuum tubes had become limitations. Putting a computer in an airplane or a missile was impossible; a better type of switch was needed.

Toward the end of the 1940s, this problem was solved by three scientists at Bell Telephone Laboratories (Bell Labs) in New Jersey. John Bardeen (1908–1991), Walter Brattain (1902–1987), and William Shockley (1910–1989) were trying to develop an amplifier that would boost telephone signals. The device they invented in late 1947—the **transistor**—turned out to have a more important use in computer switches. A single transistor was about as big as a pea and used virtually no electricity, so computers made from thousands of transistors were smaller and more efficient than those made from vacuum tubes.

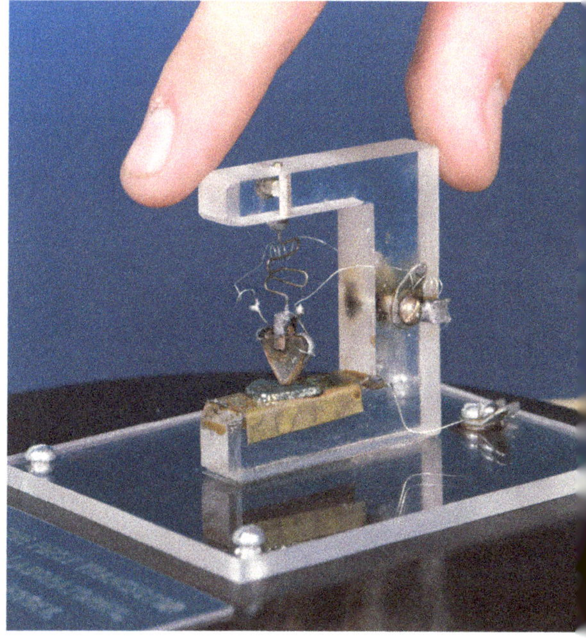

A replica of the first working transistor from 1947

Originally, transistors had to be made one at a time and then hand-wired into complex circuits. Working independently, two American electrical engineers, Jack Kilby (1923–2005) and Robert Noyce (1927–1990), devised a better way of making transistors: the integrated circuit (1958). Their idea enabled thousands of transistors—and the intricate connections between them—to be manufactured in miniaturized form on the surface of a piece of silicon, one of the chemical elements of sand.

Computers Advance

In 1943, before transistors were invented, IBM executive Thomas Watson Sr. had reputedly quipped, "I think there's a world market for about five computers." Within a decade, his own company proved him wrong—using vacuum tubes to manufacture its first general-purpose computer, the IBM 701, for twenty different customers.

Women and Computers

Men are not the only ones who have been involved in the invention of computer technologies. Many women have also contributed. For example, when Charles Babbage was devising his early mechanical computers, he was assisted by Augusta Ada Byron King (1815–1852). King, also known as Ada Lovelace, was the daughter of the English poet Lord Byron. Many describe Ada King as the world's first computer programmer because she helped Babbage to realize that his machine could be reprogrammed to do different jobs.

A century later, women were making pioneering contributions with the first electronic computers. Before the ENIAC was invented, the army used seventy-five young women who were known as "computers" to calculate its missile-firing tables. Six of them were later responsible for operating and programming the ENIAC. Adele Goldstein (1920–1964, wife of an ENIAC scientist, wrote the machine's operating manual. When the ENIAC's inventors, John Mauchly and J. Presper Eckert, formed their own corporation in the late 1940s, one of their employees was Grace Murray Hopper (1906–1992). The inventor of the computer **compiler**, Hopper had programmed the Harvard Mark I and written its technical manual. During the 1960s, perhaps the greatest achievement in computing was guiding Apollo space rockets to the moon. Some of the important Apollo programs were written by Evelyn Boyd Granville (1924–), an African American mathematician working for IBM. IBM contracted with NASA, and NASA took Granville onto its team.

The arrival of transistors changed everything, making companies such as IBM able to develop increasingly affordable business machines from the 1950s onward.

Until that decade, most of the advances in computing had come about through improvements in hardware—the mechanical, electrical, or electronic components from which computers are made. During the 1950s, advances were also made in software—the programs that control how computers operate. Much of the credit

In modern times, women are as likely as men to make brilliant computer scientists or dot-com Internet pioneers. Working at Sun Microsystems in the 1990s, Kim Polese (1961–) managed the development of Java, a powerful programming language designed for the World Wide Web. Around the same time, in Japan, Mari Matsunaga helped to launch iMode, a popular way of using the Internet on cell phones. For this achievement, she was later singled out as Asia's top businesswoman by *Forbes* magazine. Pat Sueltz began her career as a telephone linewoman in Los Angeles in the mid-1970s. Twenty years later, she was technical adviser to IBM's chief executive officer; she then became a president at Sun Microsystems, and later chief executive officer of several major Internet firms.

Many women have been encouraged to pursue careers in computing as a result of the efforts of American computer scientist Anita Borg (1949–2003). She formed an online community called Systers in 1987, which now has around four thousand women members in fifty-four countries. Until her death from brain cancer, Borg battled to change the attitude that women "have to be different or strange to get into this field."

Women continue to influence today's technological advances. Many women, such as Heather Payne, Sheryl Sandberg, and Kristen Titus, have established themselves as leaders in the technological and social media fields. Today, there are many opportunities for more women to join the technology industry and help make a difference in our growing societies.

goes to Grace Murray Hopper (1906–1992). A mathematician who divided her time between the US Navy and several large computer corporations, Hopper is remembered as a pioneer of modern computer programming. She invented the first compiler, a computer program that "translates" English-like commands that people understand into binary numbers that computers can process, in the 1950s.

Making Computing Personal

Even the invention of the transistor did not make computers affordable enough for most people. The world's first fully transistorized computer, the PDP-1 made by Digital Equipment Corporation, still cost approximately $120,000 when it was launched in 1960. Toward the end of the 1960s, however, another breakthrough was made in electronics. This breakthrough changed everything. Robert Noyce, coinventor of the integrated circuit, and Gordon Moore (1929–) formed a company called Intel in 1968. The following year, one of Intel's engineers, Marcian Edward "Ted" Hoff (1937–), developed a way of making a powerful kind of integrated circuit that contained all the essential components of a computer. It was the **microprocessor**, popularly known as a microchip or silicon chip.

Microchips were no bigger than a fingernail and, during the early 1970s, found their way into various electronic devices, including digital watches and pocket calculators. In the mid-1970s, electronics enthusiasts started using microprocessors to build their own home computers. In 1976, two California hobbyists, Steve Jobs (1955–2011) and Steve Wozniak (1950–), used this approach to develop the world's first easy-to-use personal "microcomputers": the Apple I and Apple II.

Many other companies launched microcomputers, all of them with incompatible hardware and software. Apple's machines were so successful that by 1981 IBM decided to launch its own personal computer (PC), using software developed by the young, largely unknown Bill Gates (1955–) and his then-tiny company, Microsoft. During the 1980s, most personal computers were standardized around IBM's design and Microsoft's software. This was extremely important for businesses in particular, as employees needed to be able to share information easily.

Ease-of-Use Computers

Users needed not just compatibility but also ease of operation. Most of the early computer programmers had been highly qualified mathematicians. One inventor who recognized this was American computer scientist Douglas Engelbart (1925–). During the 1960s, he pioneered a series of inventions that made computers more user-friendly—the best known of which is the computer mouse.

Engelbart's ideas were taken up in the early 1970s at the Palo Alto Research Center (PARC), a laboratory in California that was then a division of the Xerox Corporation. Xerox had made its name and fortune in the 1960s, manufacturing photocopiers invented by Chester Carlson (1906–1968) in 1938. Executives at Xerox believed the arrival of computers heralded a new "paperless" era in which photocopiers and the like might become obsolete. Consequently, Xerox began developing revolutionary, easy-to-use office computers to ensure that it could remain in business long into the future.

After visiting Xerox PARC, Apple's head, Steve Jobs, began a project to develop his own easy-to-use computer, initially called PITS (Person In The Street). This eventually evolved into Apple's popular Macintosh (Mac) computer, launched in 1984. When Microsoft incorporated similar ideas into its own Windows software, Apple was unable to stop the company, despite a lengthy court battle. The ultimate victors were computer users, who have seen an enormous improvement in the usability of computers since the mid-1980s.

Computers Meet the Modern Age

From the abacus to the PC, computers had been largely self-contained machines. That began to change in the 1980s, when the arrival of standardized PCs made connecting computers into networks easier. Businesses, schools, universities, and home users found they could use networked computers to share information more easily than ever before. More and more people connected their computers, mainly using the public telephone system, to form what is now a gigantic worldwide network of computers called the Internet.

During the late 1980s, British computer scientist Tim Berners-Lee (1955–) pioneered an easy way of sharing information over the Internet that he named the World Wide Web. Since then, the web has proved to be one of the most important communication technologies ever invented. Apart from information sharing, it has helped people create new businesses, such as the popular auction website eBay, founded by American entrepreneur Pierre Omidyar (1967–) in 1995. In addition to offering new business opportunities, the Internet is also helping computing to evolve. One notable example of this evolution is the Linux **operating system**, originally created by Finnish computer programmer Linus Torvalds (1969–) in 1991. This software was free to users, or **open source**, and developed by thousands of volunteers working together over the Internet.

Collaboration via the Internet is one of the most important aspects of modern computing. Another is convergence, a gradual coming together of computers and other communication technologies. Telephones, cameras, televisions, computers, stereos, and sound recording equipment were once entirely separate. Now, all these technologies can be incorporated into a single pocket-sized device such as a cell phone. Collaboration and convergence indicate that computer technology is continually evolving.

Designer of Early Mechanical Computers

Charles Babbage

1791–1871

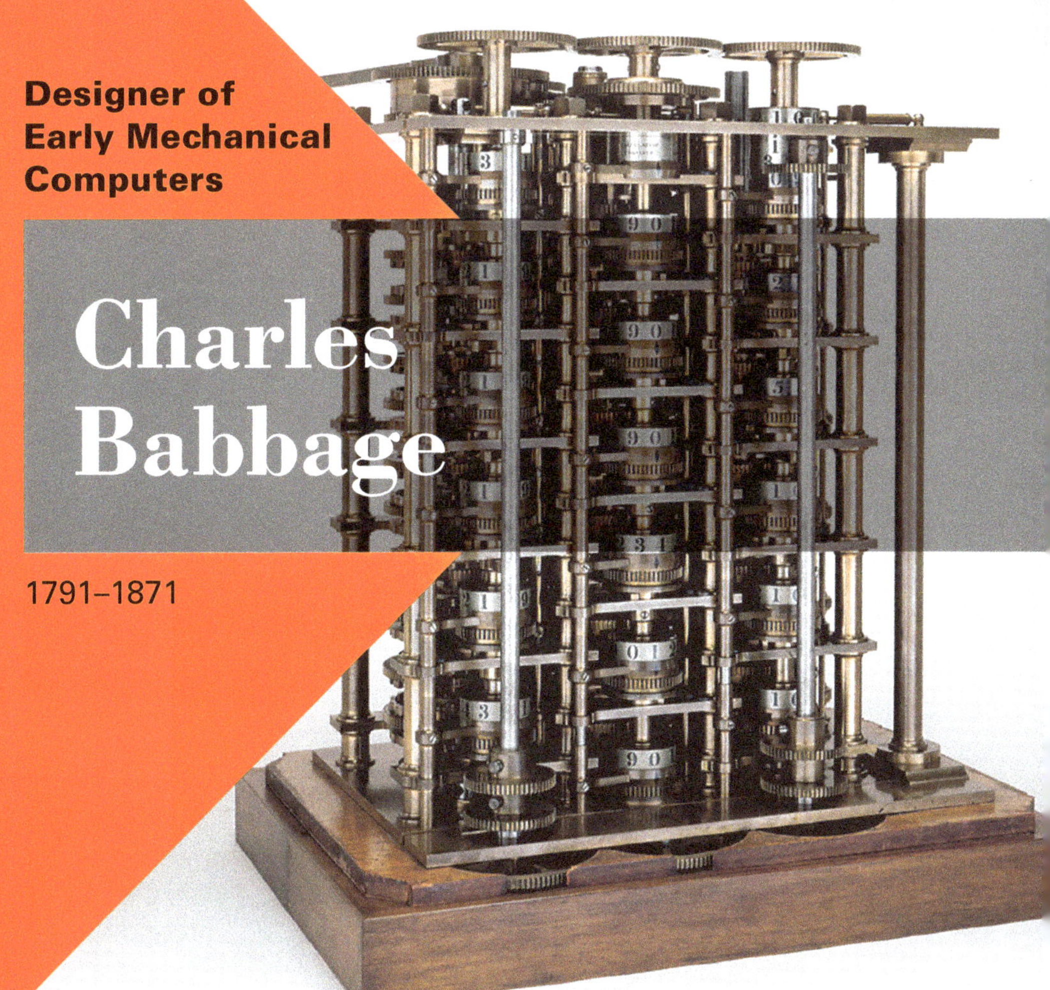

Many inventors envision their inventions when the world may not be ready for them, decades ahead of their time. When Charles Babbage designed the Analytical Engine, a complicated mechanical calculator, in the 1830s, no one knew that he had really invented an early form of the computer. His ideas were gradually forgotten, and others reinvented computers in the twentieth century. Babbage's legacy, however, lives on today, and he is acknowledged as one of the first pioneers of computing technology.

Beginnings

Charles Babbage was born in London, England, on December 26, 1791. His father, a wealthy banker, was Benjamin Babbage; his mother was Betsy Plumleigh Babbage. After several bouts of illness, Charles was sent to live in the rural coastal county of Devon in 1808, in hopes that the country air would help improve his health. Tutored at home, Babbage showed skills in mathematics and taught himself many advanced topics by reading textbooks.

In 1810, at age eighteen, Babbage entered Trinity College at Cambridge University, where he studied math. Babbage's own studies had set him far ahead of his **contemporaries**—he even knew more than some of his college tutors. He graduated from Cambridge in 1814, and that same year he married Georgiana Whitmore, with whom he had eight children (however, only three survived to adulthood).

Defining the Problem

In the twenty-first century, we rely on calculators and computers to help us with our work. In Babbage's time, people used books of mathematical tables instead. Painstakingly calculated by hand, the tables often contained errors. While Babbage was still at Cambridge, the idea came to him of making a machine that could calculate these tables automatically.

Others, including French mathematician Blaise Pascal (1623–1662) and German scientist Gottfried Leibniz (1646–1716), had already made simple calculating machines, but Babbage proposed something more advanced. He knew the method of differences technique, which uses simple additions and subtractions to calculate the answers to complex mathematical equations. His idea was to build a machine that would use gears (wheels with teeth that mesh together) to solve equations and print out the results.

Designing the Solution

By 1822, Babbage had built a working model of his Difference Engine, as he called it. He soon realized that the complete machine would be enormous and very expensive to construct because it needed thousands of separate parts, each of which had to be crafted by hand. Babbage was awarded a grant of £1,500 (about $7,500 US dollars then; approximately $180,000 US dollars in 2014) by the British government to help him proceed, but the project moved slowly and he was often distracted by other topics; during 1825, for example, he spent time researching magnetism.

Charles Babbage in 1860

In 1827, Babbage's life changed dramatically—his father, his wife, and two of his children all died that year. As a result, his health deteriorated and he took a lengthy overseas vacation to recover. More happily, he earned acclaim by publishing a book of logarithms (a simple but time-consuming way of doing calculations with mathematical tables before calculators were invented). In 1828, he was appointed Lucasian Professor of Mathematics at Cambridge, a post he would hold for the next twelve years.

Although these were great achievements, Babbage made less progress on his most important project—the Difference Engine. By the early 1830s, he had redesigned the machine and developed a printer to go with it (a separate gear-driven mechanism that could automatically print the results of calculations in neat tables). After gaining more financial help from the British government, Babbage hired a craftsman, Joseph Clement, to help him finish the project. Part of the Difference Engine was built, but construction ground to a halt when Babbage and Clement had a falling-out in 1833.

The Bigger Machine

The Difference Engine was never completed, largely because Babbage turned his attention to an even bigger project in 1834: his Analytical Engine. Unlike the Difference Engine, which could print only mathematical tables, the Analytical Engine could be programmed to make many different types of calculations. To make this possible, it was split into two pieces, a "store" (memory) to hold its results and a "mill" that could carry out complex, multistage calculations (equivalent to the processor chip in a modern computer).

Babbage's friend and supporter Augusta Ada Byron King, Countess of Lovelace (1815–1852; daughter of the English poet Lord Byron), helped him determine how to make his machine programmable. Their inspiration was an idea used in the textile-weaving loom invented by Frenchman Joseph-Marie Jacquard (1752–1834). The Jacquard loom could weave different patterns if someone fed it cards punched with holes. Different patterns of holes made the machine weave in different ways. King, who is sometimes described as the world's first computer programmer, wrote that Babbage's machines would "weave algebraic patterns just as the Jacquard loom weaves flowers and leaves."

The Analytical Engine was vastly more ambitious than the Difference Engine that Babbage had already failed to build. Indeed, modern computer scientists who have studied the plans believe it would have been as large and heavy as a small railroad locomotive. When Babbage approached the British government for more financial help, he met with little sympathy. He had already been advanced more than £17,000 (about $85,000 US dollars) to build the Difference Engine; the government had seen no return on its investment. One of Babbage's sternest critics, the Reverend Richard Sheepshanks of the Royal Astronomical Society, commented, "He was ill-judged enough to press the consideration of this new machine upon the members of government, who were already sick of the old one." Appeals to the prime minister of England fell on deaf ears, and in November 1842, the government withdrew its support.

Applying the Solution

Babbage resolved to carry on alone. However, he had spent much of his personal fortune on his projects and had no way of building either of his gigantic machines without help. In 1848, having given up hope of building the Analytical Engine, he outlined plans for another new machine, the Difference Engine No. 2. He continued to scribble thousands of pages of ideas in notebooks, most of which have now been cataloged by historians.

Reconstructing Babbage's Achievements

Although Babbage's calculators were never completed in his lifetime, attempts have been made to construct them since his death. In 1910, his youngest son, Henry Provost Babbage, used the plans of the Analytical Engine to build a hand-cranked calculator that could print its results. He also made half a dozen models of parts from the original Difference Engine.

In 1991, to commemorate the two hundredth anniversary of Babbage's birth, the Science Museum in London, England, built a partial reconstruction of the Difference Engine No. 2. Working from Babbage's original plans, the museum constructed an enormous machine consisting of about four thousand separate parts made from brass, steel, and wood, and weighing 3 tons (2.7 metric tonnes). This modern Difference Engine works more like a factory machine than the electronic calculators people use today. It is hand-cranked and can be operated by one person, although turning all its gears requires a great deal of effort and skill: the crank must turn at exactly the right speed or the gears tend to jam. To the great delight of modern engineers, it works just as Babbage had described, despite being laborious to use. In 2000, the same engineers built a reconstruction of Babbage's "computer printer."

In 2012, a charity wanting to build Babbage's Analytical Engine using his most complete print, Plan 28, began. Named after the print, the charity launched an online campaign, which gained attention in the UK and abroad. The plan is to build the Analytical Engine and display it at the Science Museum in London, before year 2030.

As Babbage aged, he became increasingly **eccentric**. Typical of the period was a paper he published in 1857, "Table of the Relative Frequency of the Causes of Breaking of Plate Glass Windows," in which he made a careful study of 464 broken windows and counted how many had been damaged by drunken people, animals, and so on. He also became fixated on noises in the street that prevented him from working and tried to have a law passed against them. His

Babbage envisioned a need for black box recorders, now standard devices for many methods of communal travel.

protests made him a figure of fun among the public: some followed and taunted him when he walked down the street, while others hired musicians with badly out-of-tune instruments to play outside his home for hours at a time. Babbage skulked inside, keeping a meticulous tally of all that annoyed him (published in his 1864 paper, "Observations of Street Nuisances"). It was in this frame of mind that Babbage died at his London home on October 18, 1871.

The Impact of the Solution on Society

Babbage's death was front-page news, but within a few years his work as an inventor was all but forgotten. In 1878, a British government committee considered whether the Analytical Engine should be built but concluded that it was not worth the effort. Babbage might have been forgotten entirely if his notebooks had not been accidentally rediscovered in 1937. At that time, mathematicians were developing advanced calculators—and the first actual computers—from electromagnetic parts, and the genius of Babbage's work became apparent. By then, however, Babbage's ideas had been reinvented. Thus, although his achievements were remarkable for their time, they did not lead directly to modern computers; for this reason, he cannot be described as the inventor of the computer.

Why were Babbage's machines never completed? They were very ambitious for their time—far more accurate than the first electromagnetic and electronic computers. Even with huge investments of public money, such complex machines might have taken decades to build. Babbage blamed the British government for its lack of vision and lack of commitment. However, in an age when no one had calculators or computers, the government had difficulty understanding just how useful Babbage's machines might have been. For his own part, Babbage seems to have been too easily distracted by other areas of study to bring his project to fruition. A poor public speaker, he was unable to present his ideas successfully. If he had managed to promote his ideas to the government more convincingly, the history of computing might have been very different.

Babbage was no failure, however. Apart from publishing six important books and around ninety scientific papers, he invented a cowcatcher (a plow for clearing cattle from railroad tracks), a type of speedometer, an improved lighthouse, improvements to the English postal system, and the Greenwich time signal. A true visionary, he saw the need for installing "black box" recorders to investigate transportation accidents and believed the world would need to exploit the power of the oceans when reserves of coal ran out. In addition to helping found scientific societies, Babbage was active in politics and ran, though unsuccessfully, for the British Parliament. His 1827 book of logarithms was in widespread use until the end of the nineteenth century. In 1832, he published *On the Economy of Machines and Manufactures*, a study of how goods could be made more efficiently. This work pioneered an important modern field known as operational research. Despite these great achievements, Babbage died a disappointed man because he never realized his great dream of building a calculating engine.

Timeline

1791
Charles Babbage born in London

1814
Babbage graduates from Cambridge

1822
Babbage constructs a working model of the Difference Engine

1834
Babbage conceives of the Analytical Engine

1842
The British government withdraws its support of Babbage's work

1871
Babbage dies in London

1991
Engineers at the Science Museum in London reconstruct Babbage's Difference Engine No. 2

2012
UK-based campaign Plan 28 tries to raise funds to build the Analytical Engine

Inventor of the World Wide Web

Tim Berners-Lee

1955–

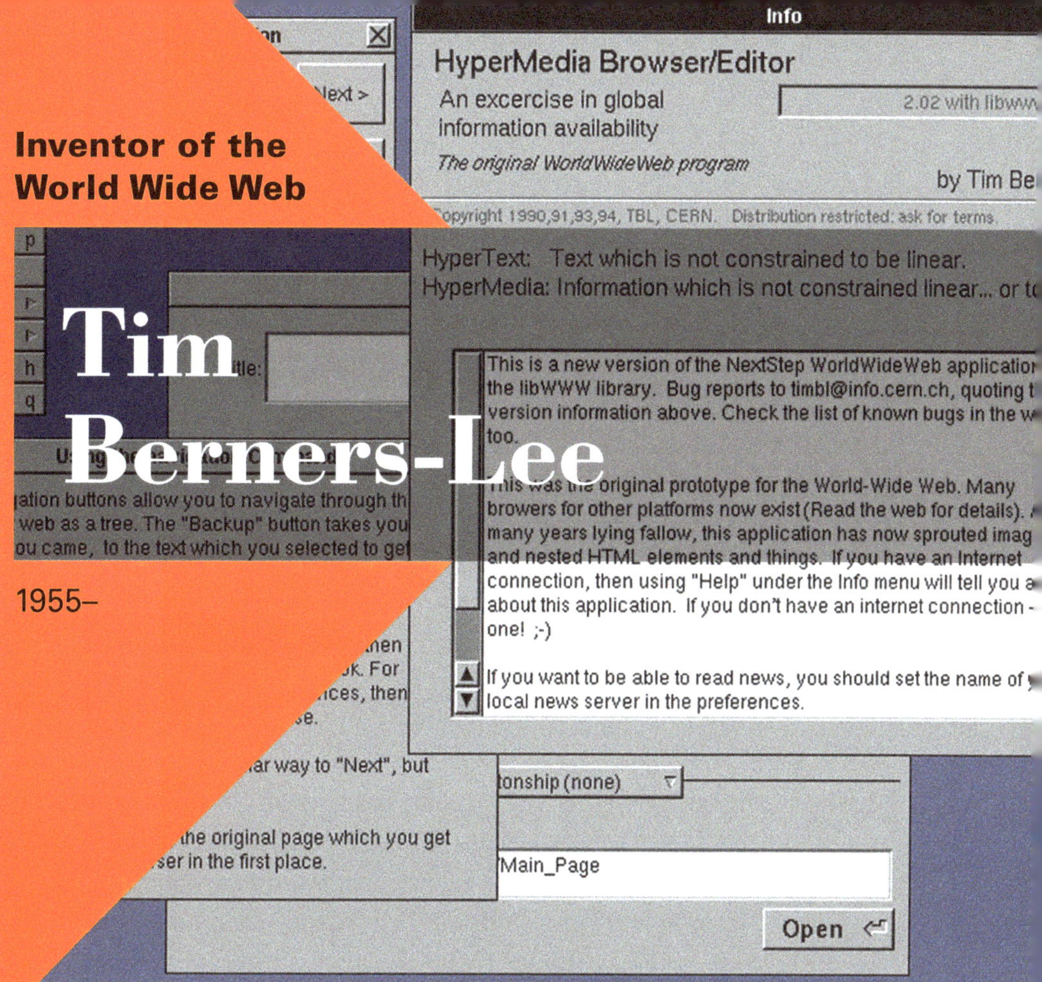

Since the early 1990s, people have been able to connect to each other from across the world using computers and computer-like devices. The first invention that made this possible was the World Wide Web. Developed in the late 1980s by Englishman Tim Berners-Lee, the World Wide Web changed the way societies interacted with one another. Today, it has more or less become a facet of everyday life, as people around the globe can receive information at the tap of a button, and many remain connected to the World Wide Web at all times.

The Start of a New Era

Born on June 8, 1955, Tim Berners-Lee was raised in London by his parents, Conway Berners-Lee and Mary Lee Woods. Both were accomplished mathematicians who had met in the English city of Manchester while working to develop one of the world's first electronic computers, the Manchester Mark I. They passed on their enthusiasm for math to their son and encouraged him to play algebraic games over breakfast. Berners-Lee believes he learned to read by touching the raised metal letters on London street signs. He also admits being shy and a "geek": he learned to tinker with electronics after discovering how to make gadgets that could control his model railroad—but electronics soon interested him more.

At Oxford University in the early 1970s, Berners-Lee studied physics, thinking it would be more useful than the math he loved. While there, he bought himself a decrepit television set for £5 ($8), took it apart, added some "junk from the Tottenham Court Road," where London's electronics stores were based, and turned it into a computer monitor. Later he added other electronic components to make a simple computer. Most of his computing experience came from sharing the university's large mainframe computer. However, when he and a friend were caught using the computer to organize social events for their college, they were immediately banned from the system.

After earning his bachelor's degree in 1976, Berners-Lee would ordinarily have continued with physics to earn a doctorate. Instead, he chose to start work for a large electronics company, Plessey Data Systems, and relocated to the harbor town of Poole, Dorset, where he could enjoy rural life and windsurf on the sea. Two years later, he joined a smaller company, D.G. Nash, and developed software for computer printers, among other accomplishments.

CERN

Then, as now, talented programmers could earn a good living working freelance on short-term contracts. In 1980, Berners-Lee moved to Switzerland to work as a contract programmer at CERN (pronounced "sern"), the European particle physics laboratory near Geneva. At

CERN, scientists search for subatomic particles (the tiny components that make up atoms) by firing atoms at other atoms so they explode into fragments. Thousands of leading scientists worked at the huge laboratory, often on temporary visits from universities around the world, but most stayed for only a year or two.

Defining the Problem

Berners-Lee soon saw a problem: there was no real way to keep track of all the information the scientists needed to share—when they left CERN, they took their knowledge, stored mostly in their heads, with them. He also found that they swapped most of their ideas not during work but during coffee breaks, where they met and chatted informally. Trying to think of a solution to let the scientists pool their knowledge, he wrote a computer program called Enquire, named for *Enquire within upon Everything*, a popular encyclopedia in Victorian times that offered a simple, quick reference to all kinds of information. The Enquire program could store different pieces of text in a database (a computerized card index), make connections (links) between different subjects, and allow different individuals to access the same information from different computers.

In 1981, Berners-Lee left CERN for three years. He returned in 1984 and again became frustrated with the problem of how groups of people can share knowledge effectively. In March 1989, he proposed reviving his Enquire system using **hypertext**, which an eccentric computer pioneer, Ted Nelson (1937–), had developed in the early 1960s. Hypertext is a way of connecting the documents on a computer system with highlighted words or phrases; clicking on one of these takes the reader to another document for more explanation. Nelson had struggled for many years to develop Xanadu, a complex hypertext system that could link together a huge collection of human knowledge.

Designing the Solution

Berners-Lee saw a much simpler way of using hypertext to solve CERN's problems. He decided that each document needed its own unique name, which he called a uniform resource locator (URL), so

Tim Berners-Lee at the Eighteenth Annual Webby Awards in May 2014

everyone could find it. Each document also needed to be written, or marked-up, in the same structured format called hypertext markup language (HTML), so all the CERN computers would know how to read and process it. Finally, all the computers would need to transfer (send and receive) documents in exactly the same way using a system called hypertext transfer protocol (HTTP). Together, all this could create a "web" of knowledge from all the documents stored on all the various computers used by the scientists. It would also have the advantage of allowing all kinds of computer systems—from the largest mainframe to the smallest PC—to share information seamlessly, something that had never really been possible before.

One piece of the puzzle was still missing—a way of reading those documents on a computer screen. In October 1990, Berners-Lee completed the puzzle when he wrote a program called WorldWideWeb for his CERN colleagues. This was the world's first web browser: a program anyone could run on a computer to access (or browse) the documents stored on others' computers.

The Worldwide Reach of the Web

WorldWideWeb proved to be a big hit at CERN and, during the summer of 1991, Berners-Lee agreed to make it available free on the Internet (the network linking computer systems around the world that was then mostly used by students and academics). On August 6, 1991, he set up the first web page at info.cern.ch, describing progress with his new invention and noting that many people outside the physics world were already using it. A vision was starting to emerge of something bigger. Soon, others were writing better web browsers and the idea of the World Wide Web, as the project became known, began to spread rapidly.

The next major development is attributed to Marc Andreessen, a University of Illinois student who began tinkering with the web in 1992. By the end of that year, he and a friend, Eric Bina, had decided to write their own web browser, which they called Mosaic and released in March 1993. Unlike other browsers, it could show images (graphics) and words (text) side by side in magazine-like pages onscreen. Mosaic was an overnight sensation and led Andreessen to develop an even more popular browser called Netscape Navigator in October 1994. Almost a year later, Microsoft Corporation finally realized that the web—a major new development in computing—might threaten its existence and hurriedly launched its own web browser, Internet Explorer. The tussles between Netscape and Microsoft soon led to a period of computer history called the browser wars, when the two companies battled for domination.

Working the Web

The web is a way of linking computers and other smart devices such as smartphones and tablets together so someone sitting at one machine can quickly read (browse) information stored on other machines. The devices that store the information are called web servers—their job is to provide information to people. The devices that want to access the information have to run programs called web browsers or clients, such as Chrome, Safari, or Mozilla Firefox.

Every page of information stored on a web server has a name, called its URL (uniform resource locator), which looks like this: http://www.mywebsiteaddress.com/mypage.html. The URL has three parts. The first part (http://) shows that the address lives somewhere on the web. Nowadays, you do not always have to include the first part when typing the address. The computer or device you are using will automatically add the http:// when it conducts its search. The second part (www.mywebsiteaddress.com) is the name of the web server where the website lives, with the ".com" part of the address showing that the website is commercial (business-related). For other groups, such as government or education, the terms ".gov" or ".edu" can be used at the end. The third part (mypage.html) is the name of the web page that is stored on that server.

When a person types a URL into a web browser, the browser splits the address into these three parts. Next, it sends a message to the web server that stores mywebsiteaddress.com and asks it for the web page mypage.html. The web server, which can be just an ordinary personal computer, laptop, or tablet, pulls this file off its hard disk (internal storage) and sends it back to the browser. Surfing a website involves an ongoing dialogue between the web browser and the server managing the site: requests for pages travel from the browser to the server; web pages, images, and other files travel back in the opposite direction.

Applying the Solution

Tim Berners-Lee watched the developments of the browser wars with concern. He wanted the web to be a place where people could work together for the common good, not something companies could take over to make a profit. The moment he had released his program on the Internet, he had given up control of the web—had that been a good idea? Andreessen had already made some changes to the original concept that Berners-Lee was not sure about. Berners-Lee thought adding automatic pictures to web pages might make the whole Internet grind to a halt because at that time images took so long to transmit. Suddenly, many companies were developing products for the web and setting up their own websites. If all these new programs and sites could not work together, the web might collapse into chaos instead of bringing people together.

The problem was difficult, and it marked a change in direction for Berners-Lee. In 1994, he left CERN to work in the computer science laboratory at the Massachusetts Institute of Technology (MIT). There, he founded an organization called the World Wide Web Consortium (W3C). This ambitious project was designed to help the web develop for the benefit of all its users by suggesting rules (called standards) that everyone would be encouraged to follow. One activity has involved helping the HTML language to evolve so that web pages will work on as many different computers as possible for as many users as possible. Like other inventors who struggle to perfect what they

Profit from Patents

One area where the World Wide Web Consortium (W3C) has been very active is in **patents** on web technology. A patent is a way for inventors to protect their creations and earn royalties (payments) from others who use them. Tim Berners-Lee has always refused to profit from the web. Rather than patent his invention, he chose to make it available to others free of cost. As W3C's director, he has championed the idea of an Internet community where others do the same for the common good.

Not everyone agrees with this philosophy. The history of invention remembers many who were driven by the desire to get rich and who succeeded. Internet inventors are no different; many people and companies are trying to take out patents for new technologies. Patents have become a controversial issue for the Internet community, where many people still expect to share things freely instead of buying them. Tim Berners-Lee has had to be a tactful diplomat, balancing the idea of the free, community web against the interests of private corporations, which want to help the web to develop but also need to make money from it.

have created, Berners-Lee has always insisted that the web is a work in progress and that it is not finished. Nobody appointed the W3C, but with Berners-Lee at the helm, it has remained the most important guiding hand behind the web's development.

Apart from the W3C, Berners-Lee's other main interest is a project called the **semantic web**. "Semantic" is another word for "meaningful"—the idea is to make websites that computers can understand without human supervision. Then, for example, if a user instructed his computer to find him a better job or a perfect home, it could automatically search many websites for the information and report back. In recent years, the semantic web has been taking shape. It is hoped that by 2020 a full version of it will be available for users.

Tim Berners-Lee receives the inaugural Queen Elizabeth Prize for Engineering in June 2013.

Honors and Awards

The University of Southampton in England, where Tim Berners-Lee works as professor of electronics and computer science, was one of the first institutions to recognize the importance of Berners-Lee's invention by awarding him an honorary degree in 1996. Since then, he has received dozens of awards and prizes from organizations worldwide. These have included a MacArthur Fellowship in 1998 and nomination as one of *Time* magazine's one hundred greatest minds of the twentieth century in 1999. In 2004, he was knighted by the queen of England and became Sir Timothy Berners-Lee; the same year, he was awarded the first Millennium Technology Prize by the people of Finland. In 2007, he won the US-based Charles Stark Draper Prize, and in 2009, he was elected a foreign associate of the National Academy of Sciences. In June of that year, he was asked to work with the UK government to make web data more open and accessible. In 2013, he was awarded the Queen Elizabeth Prize for Engineering for "groundbreaking innovation in engineering that has been of global benefit to humanity."

These awards and honors recognize the huge importance of the web, which has had a dramatic impact on society since it became hugely popular in the mid-1990s. The web has become a single point of contact for almost every kind of information and a way to reach out from the computer in the home to hundreds of millions of other computers all over the world.

The Impact of the Solution on Society

The huge importance of the web has made Berners-Lee a public figure, but a very reluctant one. He has even written an FAQ (list of frequently asked questions) so that he no longer has to say the same things to journalists repeatedly. Its final question reads, "Can you tell me more about your personal life?" The answer: "No, I can't—sorry. I like to keep work and personal life separate." Colleagues paint a picture of a man who has broad interests but still has an eye for detail; someone who can understand very complex issues like computer networks and technology patents, but never forgets that he has to keep the web simple enough for children to use. Asked how he would like to be remembered by history, he has said, "I would hope I would be remembered as just a regular ordinary person, totally full of faults just like everybody else."

The awards certainly recognize Berners-Lee's role as the "father" of the World Wide Web: a selfless inventor who opted to share his idea for free. They also recognize his continuing work as the web's guiding hand at W3C and the way he continues to devote himself to making the web better for everyone. Berners-Lee has always had a bigger vision, though he puts his ambition modestly: "The world can only really be changed one piece at a time. The art is picking that piece."

Timeline

1955
Tim Berners-Lee born

1976
Berners-Lee takes a job with Plessey Data Systems

1980
Berners-Lee makes his first proposal for a hypertext system

1990
Berners-Lee completes his program, called WorldWideWeb

1991
Berners-Lee sets up the first web page

1994
Berners-Lee founds the World Wide Web Consortium (W3C)

1998
Berners-Lee awarded a MacArthur Fellowship

2004
Berners-Lee knighted

2013
Berners-Lee receives Queen Elizabeth Prize for Engineering

Founder of Amazon

Jeff Bezos

1964–

New Mexico–born and Princeton-educated Jeffrey Preston Bezos is the founder and chief executive officer of Amazon.com, the world's largest virtual bookstore and a massive online retailer of everything from books and music to electronics, toys, and household goods. Amazon.com is one of the Internet's biggest success stories and played a pivotal role in shifting the consumer-buying model from brick-and-mortar stores to online retailers.

Growing Up Bezos

Jeff Bezos came from humble beginnings in Albuquerque, New Mexico. His teenage mother, Jacklyn Gise, was married for less than a year to his biological father, Ted Jorgensen. When Bezos was four years old, Jacklyn married Mike Bezos, a Cuban immigrant whose surname her son adopted.

Bezos was a curious child who turned his family's garage into a lab and would rig electrical contraptions around the house. He loved computers and excelled in school, graduating as valedictorian of his high school class in Miami, where the family had moved when he was a teenager. Bezos's aptitude for technology is perhaps not surprising: his maternal grandfather, with whom he spent many childhood summers, was a retired rocket scientist.

Bezos started his career as a businessman at a young age. He started his first company, Dream Institute, while he was still in high school. The institute was an educational summer camp for students in fourth, fifth, and sixth grades. It promoted creative thinking and had an extensive reading list, according to BusinessInsider.com: *The Once and Future King, Stranger in a Strange Land, Lord of the Rings.*

After high school, Bezos attended Princeton University, where he studied computer science and electrical engineering, graduating **summa cum laude** in 1986. Surprisingly, he didn't go into a technology career upon graduating. Instead, he worked at several Wall Street firms, including Fitel, Bankers Trust, and D.E. Shaw & Co., where he became the company's youngest-ever vice president in 1990. D.E. Shaw is where Bezos met his wife and the mother of his four children, MacKenzie, who is, fittingly, a novelist.

Wall Street paid well, but Bezos wanted to pursue something new. So in 1994, the thirty-year-old made a risky decision: he quit his job, moved to Seattle, and decided to open an online bookstore. Thus, retail giant Amazon.com was born.

Defining the Problem

With his technology background, Jeff Bezos had a passion for the marriage of innovation and technology. In the early days of the Internet, Bezos was researching new ventures for his employer, investment firm D.E. Shaw. He was fascinated by statistics showing the exponential growth of World Wide Web usage. An idea germinated in Bezos's mind: Why not tap into this incredible growth as a sales opportunity? The question was, in what way? Bezos made a list of potential products he thought might work well for an online retailer; along with software and CDs, books were on the list. So what made this lover of technology choose books over software or CDs? One simple answer is supply. Millions of books were in print, but brick-and-mortar stores could only logistically stock so many. However, an online bookstore could offer far greater numbers of titles. In fact, the potential for inventory was nearly limitless. Moreover, consumers could browse this inventory and purchase books at their leisure from their personal computers. Plus, books were easy to ship and hard to break, so losses due to damage were likely to be minimal.

Designing the Solution

At this point, Bezos had an idea and a goal: to be a place where readers could find and purchase millions of different books without ever leaving the comfort of their own home. Now he had to figure out how to make his vision into a reality.

Bezos, MacKenzie, and their dog left the East Coast for the Pacific Northwest. He chose Seattle as his new home base because it was a high-tech hotspot with a lot of potential talent for his new business and it was near Ingram Book Group's warehouse in Oregon. Proximity to both talent and inventory was key for Bezos's entrepreneurial vision.

What's in a Name?

Amazon.com wasn't Bezos's original name idea for his new company. He envisioned his brainchild being called Cadabra.com, as in "abracadabra." However, when he ran the name by his attorney, the attorney misheard him and asked why Bezos would want to call his company Cadaver.com. Oops! Given that Bezos's business venture wasn't in the death/funeral/morgue business, he quickly reconsidered the name. He toyed with Relentless.com and eventually came up with Amazon.com, after the meandering, second largest river in the world.

While MacKenzie drove them across the country to their new home, Bezos created his business plan for Amazon.com on his laptop and called prospective investors, eventually raising $1 million from family and friends. That was enough to rent a house in Seattle and set up the business in their garage.

Jeff Bezos unveils the Amazon Kindle DX e-reader in May 2009.

Bezos hired five employees, and the six of them spent a year working out of that garage. They learned how to source books and created an easily navigable computer interface. Ease of use was a key component of Bezos's plan: the Internet was still relatively new to many people, and the website needed to be user-friendly to even the most novice of users. The average Joe needed to be able to efficiently search for and find a book on a desired topic, making Amazon.com an irresistibly easy shopping experience compared to hunting through traditional bookstores.

Bezos also wanted Amazon.com to be a type of "virtual community." He and his team created programs for the site that allowed users to add book reviews and to find recommended books based on their previous purchases. Amazon.com needed to be like the best low-pressure salesperson ever—interested in hearing customers' feedback and quick to point them to similar books they might enjoy. Interestingly, early feedback on Amazon.com had critics writing to Bezos and asking why on earth he would allow customers to post negative book reviews on his site. After all, a negative review might convince someone *not* to buy a product; critics asserted that perhaps Bezos didn't understand his business. But Bezos maintained that they would sell *more* products if they helped people make purchasing decisions—and allowing honest reviews was one good way to help people make such decisions.

Applying the Solution

Amazon.com officially opened for business on July 16, 1995, offering more than one million titles. They were, as they said, "Earth's Biggest Bookstore." Initial response was huge and favorable—in part because one of the founders of Yahoo! liked what he saw and offered to feature Amazon.com on Yahoo!'s What's Cool page.

By the end of its first week in business, Amazon.com had pulled in $12,000 worth of orders. However, the launch wasn't without its rough spots. The small team had difficulty meeting the order demand in the first couple of weeks, even while working until two or three in the morning every day and kneeling on concrete floors to pack books because Bezos had neglected to order packing tables. Perhaps worse, they discovered a flaw in the site that allowed customers to order a negative quantity of books and receive a credit on their credit card.

Overall, people loved the huge selection at Amazon.com, the user-friendly site design, and the efficient customer service—which initially consisted of Bezos himself sitting at a table and answering customer e-mails. Customers told their friends about this new business and posted about it on Internet newsgroups and mailing lists, which drew more customers. Bezos invested very little money in advertising—the company's success was due almost solely to word-of-mouth referrals from satisfied customers. However, Bezos *did* engage in one advertising ploy: he hired mobile billboards to drive by Barnes & Noble stores with signs showing Amazon.com's web address and the question, "Can't find that book you wanted?"

Despite Bezos's overall lack of marketing and the initial rough spots after the launch, in a little over a year, Amazon.com had one hundred employees and more than $15 million in sales. By 1999, just four years after its launch, it had more than three thousand employees worldwide and more than $610 million in sales. By 2014, the company's annual revenue was approximately $75 billion.

Barnes & Noble, the large brick-and-mortar bookstore, was an initial competitor. It launched an online presence and claimed to have twice the book inventory of Amazon.com. However, by this time Bezos had expanded Amazon.com's offerings to include CDs, which proved to be a lucrative additional market. No longer simply "Earth's

Biggest Bookstore," Amazon.com was now "Books, Music, and More." The "and More" included toys, games, pharmacy items, and consumer electronics and has continued to grow.

The Impact of the Solution on Society

Amazon.com was the first phenomenally successful Internet shopping site. It has become the template for online shopping platforms. Countless online retailers have designed their sites to mimic Amazon.com's functionality and usability. Customer product reviews, which were a very early feature on Amazon.com, are mainstays of virtually every online retail site now.

On a less positive note, Amazon.com has had a detrimental effect on brick-and-mortar stores—particularly bookstores. It's not uncommon for people to wander into a bookstore and browse, but then purchase any books they're interested in from Amazon.com, where they can get the book for less money and delivered to their doorstep within a couple of days. Many mom-and-pop bookstores, already suffering from competition by bookstore giants such as Barnes & Noble, have been driven out of business by Amazon.com. Even Barnes & Noble struggles now, in the face of huge competition from Amazon.com.

It's true that Amazon.com has changed our entire retail business model. People are abandoning brick-and-mortar stores for the convenience and prices afforded by Amazon.com. Yet it's hard to fault Jeff Bezos for this. He simply saw a need and a potential new market, and built his empire on it—to the tune of a net worth of almost $30 billion, at most recent estimate. Furthermore, even though brick-and-mortar retailers have suffered at the hands of Bezos's brainchild, at the same time online retailers have been able to flourish, thanks to the path paved by Amazon.com.

Bezos is never content to simply rest on his success, though. Amazon.com stepped beyond traditional print books and into e-books and audiobooks. The Amazon Kindle is a phenomenally successful e-reader introduced in late 2007 and frequently updated since. The Fire HDX is a Wi-Fi–enabled tablet that competes with the Apple iPad. In addition to CDs and vinyl, Amazon.com offers digital music downloads. It has expanded into streaming media content with its

Many new computing devices, like this Kindle Fire tablet, are entering the market.

Amazon Prime Instant Video. It now offers **cloud** storage via Amazon Cloud Drive and features an app store for Android devices. Some of its latest offerings are Fire TV, which is a set-top box that allows viewers to stream media content, and the Fire Phone, which features a 3-D display and is a competitor to Apple's iPhone.

How does one company manage to do so many things—and do them well? Having a strong team is a major key to success, but a strong team also needs a strong leader, and Bezos certainly fits that role. He has been described as cajoling, quirky, fun, and inspiring, but also irritating, demanding, and micromanaging. Bezos isn't necessarily the easiest leader to work for, but he is indisputably brilliant in his business sense. He remains determined to maximize every bit of usefulness of his site. For example, he pioneered 1-Click ordering and quickly secured a patent so that no other online retailer can feature a one-click buying option without paying a royalty to Amazon.com. He also filed a patent for a feature that allows movement recognition as an input mechanism—meaning that, theoretically, Amazon.com customers will be able to purchase items simply by nodding their heads while on the site. In a somewhat surprising move in 2013, Bezos bought the *Washington Post*, which he plans to turn into a national publication that will be featured on the Kindle Fire tablet.

It's anyone's guess what Bezos's next great idea for Amazon.com will be, but one thing is for sure: the online shopping site is here to stay and has forever changed the way we do business.

Timeline

1964
Jeffrey Preston Bezos born in Albuquerque, New Mexico

1986
Bezos graduates Princeton University with degrees in computer science and electrical engineering

1990
Bezos becomes D.E. Shaw & Co.'s youngest-ever vice president

1994
Bezos moves to Seattle, Washington, with plans to create Amazon.com

1995
Amazon is formally launched in July

2007
Bezos unveils the Kindle, Amazon.com's e-reader

2013
Bezos purchases the *Washington Post*

Inventor of the Modern Calculator

William Seward Burroughs

1857–1898

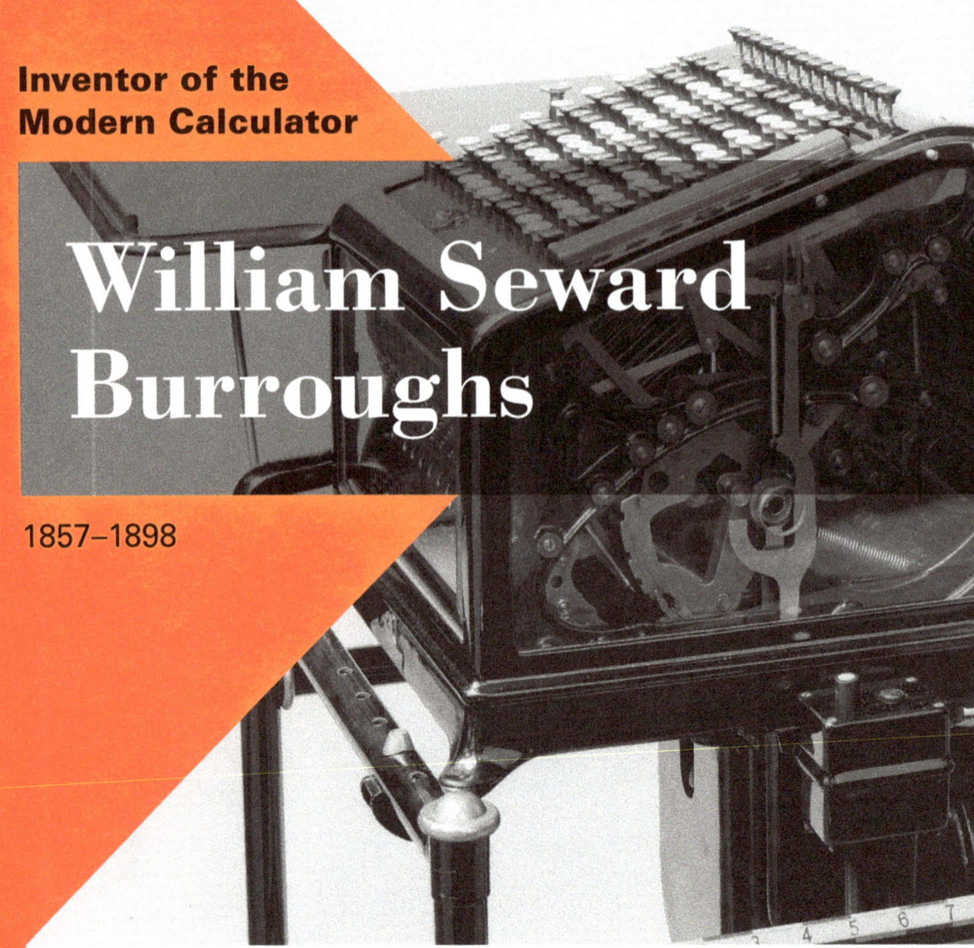

Some inventors create their inventions from original ideas. Others use already existing ideas from other people, improve upon them, and make the updated product their own. William Burroughs was not the first person to realize that a machine could compute tedious sums, but he revolutionized the business world by creating an adding machine that was reliable, practical, and easy to use.

An Inventor Is Born

Born in 1857, William Seward Burroughs grew up in Auburn, a town in central New York. His father was a mechanic and amateur inventor. Burroughs left school when he was a teenager, and, although he was interested in mechanics, he eventually went to work in a bank as a clerk. In 1879, he married Ida Selover; the couple had four children, and one of Burroughs's grandchildren, William Seward Burroughs II (1914–1997), became a well-known poet and novelist.

Three years after his marriage, Burroughs was plagued by ill health, most probably caused by tuberculosis. His doctors suggested that he move to a warmer climate and take up more physically active work. In his job at the bank, Burroughs spent long hours sitting, looking over bank **ledgers** and searching for mistakes. The work was necessary—at the time, calculations were done by hand, with the resulting numbers being copied into the ledgers by hand also. Mistakes were all too common, no matter how much care was taken by bank employees.

His doctors were convinced that all that time spent examining ledgers was damaging Burroughs's health. Taking their advice, Burroughs moved to St. Louis, Missouri, and went to work as an engineer.

Defining the Problem

After moving to St. Louis, Burroughs began to think about developing a machine that would perform the mathematical addition needed by banks. A machine seemed ideal for the job. The math was not complicated; it just involved adding numbers—thus such a machine would not be too complex to build. Bookkeepers and clerks at the time were trained to add accurately and quickly in their heads, but even well-trained people had moments of inattention. A machine, in contrast, would never get tired or distracted.

Burroughs was far from the first person to realize that machines could be used for calculations; the abacus, an ancient counting machine using beads, was invented around 500 BCE. Adding machines were first built in the 1600s by people looking for help with the math needed in astronomy or finance. These machines, however, were essentially playthings—they were idiosyncratic, delicate, and often so difficult to use that only their inventors could make them work. They were certainly impractical for a business concern like a bank, where many different people performed calculations.

Burroughs wanted to devise something that would be easy to use and would contain built-in safeguards to help prevent errors. One such

William S. Burroughs invented the Burroughs calculator.

safeguard, which he envisioned early on, would be a printout: his machine would print the numbers as they were added and print the final sum, all onto a roll of paper. That would help prevent errors caused by inaccurate copying of figures.

Building such a machine would take money, however—something Burroughs did not have. One day in 1884, he was sent on a job to a store in St. Louis, and he began discussing his ideas for an adding machine with an employee. The employee became so intrigued by Burroughs's idea that he promised to invest and to gain the support of some of his friends, too.

Soon, Burroughs had capital of about $300 to use in developing his machine. One of the first things he did with the money was to rent a space in a workshop from Joseph Boyer, a sympathetic machinist.

Designing the Solution

Burroughs applied for a patent on the basic workings of his machine in 1885. The next year, he and his investors founded the American Arithmometer Company. ("Arithmometer" was a popular term at the time for what is now called a calculator. The word "calculator", in contrast, originally referred to a person who performed mathematical calculations, not a machine.) Burroughs was named vice president.

Burroughs wanted his machine to be exactly right before offering it for sale. His investors, however, had provided him with much-needed funds because they expected him to produce a practical machine and pay back their investment. Adding to the pressure to speed development of the machine was the introduction in 1887 of a competing machine, the Comptometer, devised by the Chicago inventor Dorr E. Felt.

In 1888, American Arithmometer began production of Burroughs's adding machine. The machine had a numerical keypad as well as a lever on the side. A user would enter numbers using the keypad and then pull the lever after each entry. To get a total, the user pulled the lever twice.

Applying the Solution

By 1890, American Arithmometer had manufactured fifty machines, and the company made its first shipment to customers. It immediately became clear, however, that the machine, which cost $475 (a substantial amount at that time), did not work.

In essence, the machine was too delicate. Burroughs had relied on gears to record the numbers entered in order to total the final sum. If someone pulled the lever with too much force, the recording gears would shake out of place. The machine might print a number correctly when it was entered, but by the time an entire column of numbers was entered and totaled, the lever had been pulled several times, the recording gears had been jostled, and the machine would give the wrong answer.

Burroughs himself had the knack of pulling the lever correctly, but he had built exactly what he had not intended to build—an adding machine that only he could use. His company recalled the machines, and he frantically went to work to improve them.

After three days of nonstop work, Burroughs hit upon a solution. The lever moved back into place because of a spring, and Burroughs surrounded the spring with a chamber filled with oil. The thick oil acted as a shock absorber, cushioning the movement of the spring. As a result, the lever moved smoothly back into place instead of snapping back, and the gears were not knocked out of place.

In 1891, the company shipped out the new machines, which customers found worked well. To celebrate, Burroughs went to a company storeroom containing the fifty recalled machines and threw each one of them out the window so that they smashed onto the ground below, saying, "I have ended the last of my troubles." Despite his euphoria, the new technology took time to catch on and replace human computers. In 1895, the company sold only 284 machines. Over the next five years, annual sales increased to almost 1000 machines.

Burroughs did not live to see his machine become widely popular, however. His health worsened, and in 1897 he retired from American Arithmometer to move to a still warmer climate. He died the next year in Citronelle, Alabama.

The Impact of the Solution on Society

Burroughs's death at age forty-one seemed to spur his associates to make his invention a success. In 1902, Boyer, who had once rented space in his shop to Burroughs, became president of American Arithmometer, a position he would hold for the next eighteen years. In 1904, Boyer changed the company's name to the Burroughs Adding Machine Company to honor the inventor.

By that point, the company employed more than a thousand people and had grown so quickly that it had moved its operations from St. Louis to a larger facility in Detroit, Michigan, the year before. In 1905, the Burroughs Company sold 7,804 machines.

The Burroughs Company was benefiting from a larger trend in American business: the growing population of the United States, combined with industrialization, was making the country's financial workings far more complex. A factory might employ thousands of people, resulting in an equal number of wages to calculate and pay. Growing incomes created more demands for financial services, and banks and insurance companies suddenly had a great deal more business to process. The workload was becoming too much for human calculators to handle. Companies faced with the prospect of having to hire hundreds or even thousands of clerks began investing in the new adding machine technology as a solution.

By the 1910s, the Burroughs Company dominated the adding machine market. The Burroughs machine had a good reputation for quality and customer service—salespeople underwent a four-week training program so that they could easily answer any questions. The company expanded its product line to include dozens of different machines, including ones that could perform mathematical functions beyond addition.

During the next few decades, the Burroughs Company, which sold its millionth machine in 1926, seemed entrenched as the dominant calculator company. However, the industry changed with the widespread introduction of computers in the 1940s, and the firm was forced to adjust. The company entered the computer market in the early 1950s, changing its name to the Burroughs Corporation in 1953 to reflect its wider product line. Like many other computer firms, Burroughs was at first largely eclipsed by International Business Machines (IBM), but the company carved a niche for itself serving banks and government entities.

Today, Burroughs's company still exists as part of the Unisys Corporation.

In 1986, Burroughs Corporation merged with Sperry Corporation to form Unisys Corporation. To date, Unisys is a multibillion-dollar company specializing in information technology consulting, and it is one of the largest technology consultants to the US government.

Information technology may seem far removed from the levers and gears Burroughs developed to help bank clerks add quickly and accurately. Burroughs's machine, however, was an enormous boon to the businesses—and the economy—of the early twentieth century, allowing firms to scale up to meet the demands of a growing population. Burroughs also took a canny approach to his technology by designing it to meet the needs of a specific industry, which not only improved his technology's marketability but also made businesses more receptive to new technology in the future.

Timeline

1857
William Seward Burroughs born in Auburn, New York

1882
Burroughs moves to St. Louis, Missouri, to work as an engineer

1884
Burroughs finds an investor to fund the development of an adding machine

1886
Burroughs and his investors found the American Arithmometer Company

1888
American Arithmometer begins production of Burroughs's adding machine

1897
Burroughs retires from American Arithmometer Company

1898
Burroughs dies

Inventor of the First Search Engine

Alan Emtage

1964–

When you go to your web browser to search for a website or keyword, you may not think much about how a search engine like this was first created or who was behind its creation. In the 1970s, computers were just starting to gain popularity, and by the late 1980s it was clear that personal computers were the way of the future. One man named Alan Emtage is credited with creating the first search engine, Archie, in 1989. He and two colleagues, Bill Heelan and J. Peter Deutsch, created it while attending McGill University in Montreal, Canada. Archie paved the way for future search engines such as Google and Safari to be created. It was one of the landmarks of the modern technological era and left a mark on the history of the computer.

Encouraged to Question and Discover

Emtage was born in 1964 in Barbados. He graduated at the top of his high school class and received the prestigious Barbados Scholarship, which is given out by the country's Ministry of Education, Science, and Innovation. He got his first computer in 1981 and immediately realized its potential.

Emtage was raised in an extended family that instilled in him a strong curiosity for the natural world and a "capacity for discovering stuff." His mother's aunts were particularly influential in his life. His aunt Constance was a science teacher and headmaster. She encouraged him to listen to the BBC's science programs and took him fishing on the seawall near the family's home at Carlisle Bay, where they'd discuss and analyze what they saw and caught. Emtage remembers her once waking him at three in the morning to witness a comet. In secondary school he followed the science track, pursuing math, physics, and chemistry, and took an interest in computers fairly early on.

Alan Emtage spends much of his time traveling the world and helping communities.

In 1986, Emtage graduated from McGill University in Montreal, Canada, with an honors bachelor's degree in computer science, followed by a master's degree in 1991. In 1989, while a student and working as a systems administrator for the School of Computer Science, Emtage and colleagues invented Archie (named for "archive" without the "v") to help him more easily find software, books, and information for students within large volumes of archives. The Archie program allowed users to search for the information they needed. It downloaded the directory listings of all the relevant files located on public anonymous FTP (file transfer protocol) sites, creating a searchable database of file names, but it did not extract pertinent words out of the content.

"Rather than spending my time logging on to FTP sites and trying to figure out what was on them, I wrote some computer scripts that would do the same thing, and much faster, too," Emtage said. He was also part of the team that brought the first Internet link to eastern Canada in 1986.

To say that Archie was a success is an understatement. Within months, half the Internet traffic to Canada was going to the innovator's machine! It was clear that Internet users longed for some way to make sense of the voluminous amount of data on the Internet and more easily find what they were seeking. The search engine was born, and it would lead to a whole new way of using and marketing to the Internet. Search engines have made the Internet a lot more convenient and fun to use, and they have allowed businesses to more readily make money from the Internet.

Defining the Problem

Before web search engines existed and the web was in its infancy, there existed a complete list of all web servers, which was constantly updated and maintained by Tim Berners-Lee. It was hosted on the CERN web server. As more and more web servers appeared, the central list could not keep up. New servers were then announced under the title "What's New!" but the complete listing was no longer posted, as it had become too enormous. It was becoming clear that some better way of sorting and indexing the information on the Internet, as well as notifying users about it, was necessary.

Designing the Solution

It was around this time that Emtage developed Archie for searching FTP archives, and it quickly caught the attention of Canadian Internet users. Although Archie was nice for searching the relatively "small" volumes and archives, it did not have the capability of "indexing" (or sorting and cataloging) the results that were returned. Archie was used with a relatively small amount of data, and the results could easily be viewed and sorted manually. However, this was not the case with the large and exponentially growing amount of data on the

Internet. Once a program that could index results came on the scene, two new search engines that included the indexing capability were created. Those were Veronica and Jughead, following the naming convention of characters in the *Archie* comic series. At least conceptually, they proved that incredibly large volumes of data could be searched, archived, and indexed in a user-friendly manner.

Applying the Solution

The next hurdle was to develop a search program that could find, parse, and return results on the graphic-based World Wide Web, rather than just the Internet. In the summer of 1993, no search engine existed for the web, although many specialized catalogues were maintained manually. Oscar Nierstrasz at the University of Geneva wrote a series of scripts that periodically "mirrored" these manually maintained pages and rewrote them into a standard format. This formed the basis for W3Catalog, the web's first primitive search engine, released on September 2, 1993. It was retired in 1996.

The next five years—from 1993 to 1998—were a fertile time for web search development. During that time, WebCrawler, Lycos, AltaVista, Yahoo!, Ask Jeeves (now called ask.com), and Dogpile were all conceived to various success. WebCrawler, released in 1994, was one of the first "all text" crawler-based search engines. Unlike its predecessors, it allowed users to search for any word in any web page, the method that has become the standard for all major search engines since. Lycos, which was released in 1994 by Carnegie Mellon University, proved that search engines could be commercially successful.

This frenzied activity culminated in Google being developed in 1998 by Larry Page and Sergey Brin while they were PhD students at Stanford University. Google adopted the idea of selling search terms in 1998 from a small search engine company named goto.com. This move had a significant effect on the search engine business, which went from struggling to being one of the most profitable businesses on the Internet. In fact, the search engine industry currently earns $780 billion annually. Of course, Emtage sees none of that money because he did not patent his original ideas behind Archie. "At the time, nobody was making money off of the Internet, and we didn't patent

How Do Search Engines Work?

So you might wonder just how web search engines work. Well, they store information about many web pages, which they cull from the HTML markup of the pages. These pages are gathered together by a web crawler (sometimes also known as a "spider"), which is an automated robot that follows every link on the site and prepares them for indexing.

The search engine then reviews the information on each page to determine how it should be indexed (for example, words can be extracted from the titles, page content, headings, or special fields called meta tags). The indexing information is stored in an index database for use in user queries. Some search engines, such as Google, store all or part of the source page (called a cache) as well as information about the web pages, whereas others, such as AltaVista, store every word of every page they find.

When a user enters a query into a search engine, typically by using keywords, the search engine looks through the index it created and provides a listing of the best-matching web pages according to its criteria, typically including a short description of the returned results.

any of the original ideas behind Archie," he reports. "The patents would have been where I would have made the money."

The Impact of the Solution on Society

Search engines have no doubt provided a great service to society. Without them we could not say that we have all the data on the web at our fingertips. Although that might still be true, we wouldn't be able to find it!

There is also no doubt that search engines have made the web a lot more convenient and fun to use. They have allowed businesses to more readily make money from the results returned. The search engine model has become so ubiquitous that we use the newly formed verb "to Google," meaning to find something on the web.

One troubling question that some professionals continue to ask is whether having so much information at our immediate fingertips is detrimental to us in any way. Various studies have been conducted to pose and answer such questions. As an example, a study by the journal *Science* in 2014 suggested a negative correlation between memory retention and search engine use. Basically, people who believed that certain data would be saved somewhere were less likely to remember it. The research also found that people have been trained to look to the Internet first for knowledge.

All computer devices today include search engines, a legacy of Alan Emtage and Archie.

These studies shouldn't have us running to the hills to live out our lives in old dilapidated cabins without electricity, but they should give us pause. As with any technological obsession in use today, sometimes it's best to take a break and go outside!

Emtage's Continuing Legacy

Since his groundbreaking work creating Archie, Alan Emtage became a founding member of the Internet Society. He went on to create and chair several working groups at the Internet Engineering Task Force (IETF), the group that sets the standards for the Internet. He has also spoken and lectured around the world on Internet information systems and the impact of the Internet on society.

He is currently chief technical officer at Mediapolis, Inc., a web engineering company in New York City that he founded with his two business partners fifteen years ago. Although he still enjoys working with computers, his passions are traveling and photography. As much as he can, he works on his mission to "witness and photographically document threatened and disappearing environments before mankind alters them irrevocably." To date, his travels have taken him to the polar regions and to every continent. Emtage has presented his photographs in several group exhibitions. His modesty and humility are still evident in how he sees his past: "I don't feel like a father of anything; it's not how I think of myself, really. I wrote a piece of **code** that gave birth to a multi-billion dollar industry," he stated in 2013 during a video interview with the *Huffington Post*. "I didn't make any money off of it, but I wouldn't change anything."

Timeline

1964
Alan Emtage born in Barbados

1986
Emtage graduates with a BA from McGill University in Montreal, Canada

1989
Emtage and colleagues invent Archie

1991
Emtage receives his master's degree in computer science

1993
Oscar Nierstrasz at the University of Geneva creates W3Catalog

1998
Larry Page and Sergey Brin found Google

2001
Google introduces a way to search through the billions of images published online

2009
Microsoft launches its rebranded search engine, called Bing

Inventor of the Computer Mouse

Douglas Engelbart

1925–2013

As computers became smaller, more accessible, and more affordable, more people began to use them. By the end of the 1970s, these once complex machines had found their way into homes, schools, and businesses. Nothing short of a revolution, this was largely the work of pioneers such as Douglas Engelbart, an American computer scientist who developed many ways of making computers more user-friendly. His most famous invention is the computer mouse.

A Pioneer by Birth

Douglas Carl Engelbart was born on January 20, 1925, in Portland, Oregon. His grandparents had been pioneer settlers. His childhood was spent on a farm in the harsh years of the Great Depression, milking cows and looking after chickens. In 1942, he graduated from high school and then entered Oregon State University, where he was an honors student in his senior year and earned a bachelor of science degree in electrical engineering.

Like many others, Engelbart found his studies interrupted by World War II. From 1944 through 1946, he served in the navy in the Philippines. With his background in electrical engineering, he made an ideal electronic technician, helping to maintain radar (a radio device ships and airplanes used to navigate) and sonar (a navigation device, based on sound waves, used on ships and submarines). Engelbart realized, as he watched how radar operators used their equipment—sitting in front of giant television-like cathode-ray tube (CRT) displays—that he was witnessing something very important about the links between humans and the complex machines they were operating.

Defining the Problem

When the war ended, Engelbart returned to his studies, graduating in 1948. He then moved to the San Francisco area and took a job with the National Advisory Committee for Aeronautics, the forerunner of the National Aeronautics and Space Administration (NASA). Around 1950, at age twenty-five, he had a sudden moment of panic. As he recalled later, he had a good job and he was about to get married—and he wondered, what was there left to achieve? As he contemplated what to do with the rest of his life, he had a vision of the future: "I got an image of myself sitting at a big CRT screen with all kinds of symbols on it, new and different ones, manipulated by a computer that could be operated through various input devices." There and then he began to form what he later called his "crusade": to redesign computer-based equipment in a way that would truly improve human lives.

He quit his job the following year and enrolled as a graduate student at the University of California at Berkeley. Over the next few

Douglas Engelbart with the first version of his computer mouse and a real mouse

years, he studied for his doctorate in electrical engineering; the work he did in this period enabled him to apply for nineteen patents on electronic equipment. By 1955, he was an assistant professor, full of what he called "wild ideas" for using new technology. One of his colleagues quietly advised that if he kept on promoting these ideas he would stay an assistant professor forever. Engelbart decided he should relocate to where his creativity and vision would be appreciated. Stanford University and the Hewlett-Packard Company both turned down his request to work in computing because, at that time, they felt computers had little future.

Designing the Solution

In 1957, Engelbart joined Stanford Research Institute (SRI). Within a few years, he had his own group, which he later named the Augmentation Research Center. The group's unusual name came from a pioneering proposal, *Augmenting Human Intellect*, that Engelbart wrote in 1962. In it, he imagined creative people such as architects sitting at CRT displays and manipulating what they could see on the screen with "a small keyboard and various other devices." The idea was to use computer technology to extend (augment) what people could do with their brains (human intellect).

During the 1960s, Engelbart and his growing team (eventually forty-seven people) set about turning this vision into reality. Beginning in 1962, they developed a user-friendly computer system called NLS (short for oNLine System), which pioneered most of the easy-to-use technologies that people today take for granted. They filed a patent for the most famous of these—the computer mouse—in 1967. It was granted in November 1971.

Applying the Solution

On December 9, 1968, Engelbart and seventeen of his colleagues attended the Fall Joint Computer Conference in San Francisco and gave a ninety-minute demonstration of their work. Around one thousand of the world's leading computer scientists were present in the hall, and they sat in silence, astonished, as Engelbart showed off a series of groundbreaking innovations. Apart from the mouse, the group presented videoconferencing (the ability to talk to colleagues by means of a computer screen), onscreen word processing (at that time, all documents were edited on paper), collaborative working (in which several people could use their mice to control a single computer screen), hypertext (a way of linking documents together, later made popular by the World Wide Web), windows (multiple documents open on the same screen at one time), and a "chordal" keyboard that let people type any letter with the fingers of just one hand. Some years later, Engelbart vividly recalled the audience reaction: "I looked up and everyone was standing, cheering like crazy."

"Yes, [Engelbart] is outdated. He's a thousand years ahead of his time." —Patrick Lincoln, head of computer science at SRI

The Impact of the Solution on Society

Of all these inventions, Engelbart was able to patent only the mouse: the others were mostly software (programming) innovations, and lawyers had deemed they could not be protected under patent law. His ideas were soon being adapted and developed elsewhere. In the 1970s, members of the SRI team went to work at the Xerox Company's Palo Alto Research Center, which incorporated some of Engelbart's ideas into a $40,000 workstation—the Alto. Although never a commercial success, this machine inspired Steve Jobs, one of the founders of Apple Computer, to develop his easy-to-use Macintosh in the early 1980s. The Macintosh, in turn, strongly influenced the "look and feel" of Microsoft Windows in the 1990s. Thus, Douglas Engelbart's work

Creating the Mouse

Early computers had no screens, keyboards, or mice. At that time computers were expensive and complex, and operating them was a skilled and time-consuming job. When Douglas Engelbart worked as a radar technician, he realized that people instinctively looked at things, pointed at them, and moved them with their hands. Engelbart wanted computers to be that easy to use, too.

The computer mouse is the most famous result of Engelbart's work. It was originally called an "X-Y position indicator for a display system." However, this technical jargon was quickly forgotten when someone noticed that the cable hanging from the front of the device looked like a mouse's tail. The original mouse had a wooden case and two wheels inside that could roll along at right angles. As the operator moved the mouse, either or both wheels turned to a small degree. An electronic circuit inside measured the wheel movements and sent this information down the cable to the computer. A program running in the computer calculated how much to move the cursor on the screen.

Douglas Engelbart remembers making his first designs for the mouse in 1961. It has changed relatively little over the intervening years. Some mice still work mechanically, like the original. They typically have a heavy rubber ball underneath that turns two small wheels hidden inside the plastic case. Newer mice use an optical system instead. A bright light-emitting diode (LED) shines red light down from the mouse onto the desk. The light reflects back into a light-detecting component (photocell). As the mouse moves, the pattern of reflected light changes. Using this information, an electronic circuit inside the mouse calculates how to move the cursor onscreen. Likewise, some mice are wireless, meaning they are not attached to the computer by a tail, but rather communicate with a small device inserted into the computer's USB holder. This allows people to control the mouse from farther distances.

In the future, computers may have built-in scanning devices that recognize people's eye movements. Instead of pointing with a mouse, the user will simply look at part of the screen and the cursor will move straight there.

helped to make several generations of computer systems easier to use from the 1970s onward.

For Engelbart himself, however, things turned out less fortunate. He received no royalties from inventing the mouse, and even SRI made little money from the invention. When the company licensed it to Apple, SRI was paid just $40,000 for a device that now sits on virtually every desk in the world. Perhaps the main reason for this failure to profit was that the mouse was about twenty years ahead of its time when it was first developed. Engelbart's original patent expired in 1977, several years before the mouse really caught on as a computer control device.

In 1977, SRI sold NLS and Engelbart's laboratory to another company, Tymshare, Inc., and funding was cut sharply. In the mid-1980s, Tymshare was bought out by the giant McDonnell Douglas Corporation, which closed down Engelbart's laboratory altogether in 1989. It was one of the more eventful years of Engelbart's life: the same year, his house burned down while he and his family stood outside, watching helplessly. Undeterred by these setbacks, in 1989, Engelbart and his daughter Christina founded the Bootstrap Institute (now called the Doug Engelbart Institute) to promote his ideas and to encourage others to work through problems intelligently.

Douglas Engelbart and former US president Bill Clinton in the Oval Office

Lasting Legacy

When the Apple Macintosh and Microsoft Windows became popular in the mid-1980s, people finally started to recognize Engelbart as a true pioneer of user-friendly computing. From the late 1980s, he received many honors and awards, such as the IEEE John von Neumann Medal, the Lemelson-MIT Prize, and the Turing Award in 1997. In 1998, he was inducted into the National Inventors Hall of Fame. Two years later, President Bill Clinton awarded him the National Medal of Technology for "creating the foundations of personal computing." Although he never received royalties for his role in bringing the mouse to the computer industry, his invention remains a prominent aspect of the digital age and the use of a computer.

The man of these many great ideas and inventions died on July 2, 2013, at the age of eighty-eight.

Timeline

1925
Douglas Carl Engelbart born in Portland, Oregon

1944
Engelbart serves in the US Navy as an electronic technician

1957
Engelbart joins the Stanford Research Institute

1971
Engelbart's team receives patent for computer mouse

1989
Engelbart founds the Bootstrap Institute

2000
Engelbart awarded National Medal of Technology

2013
Engelbart dies

Cofounder of Microsoft

Bill Gates

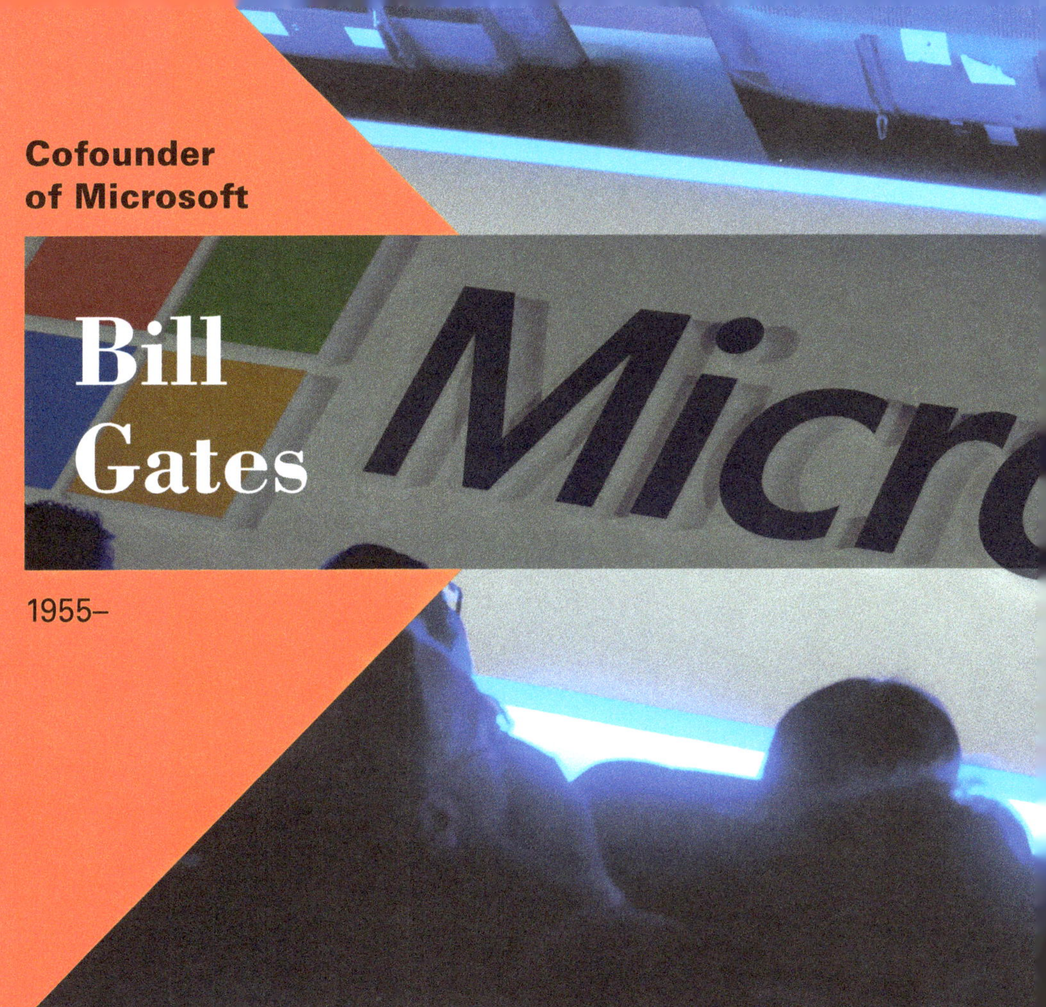

1955–

In today's history of technology, there are key players who influence major trends and make their mark on technological advancements with new and innovative ideas. One such person is Bill Gates, cofounder of one of the world's largest technological companies, Microsoft. His story is one of success, wealth, and generosity. Based on the success of his company and its creations, and his continued presence in philanthropy, it's clear that society will continue to reap the benefits of Gates's talents and drive for many years to come.

Bill Gates in May 2014

Talent Meets Opportunity and Luck

William H. Gates III was born in Seattle, Washington in 1955, the only son of William H. Gates Sr., an attorney, and Mary Maxwell Gates, an outgoing socially minded joiner. Having two sisters, he was the middle child. The Gates children grew up in a wealthy, competitive family environment.

In the Gates household, all three children were encouraged to do their best at everything they tried. Bill loved playing board games such as Risk and Monopoly and was competitive in all his endeavors. He had a very close relationship with his mother, who was outgoing, athletic, and involved in civic affairs. She stayed home to raise the children and also served in community roles and on several corporate boards, including the First Interstate Bank in Seattle (founded by her grandfather), the United Way, and International Business Machines (IBM). She often took Bill with her when she volunteered in the community.

When he was thirteen, Gates's parents had him transferred to the prestigious private Lakeside School in Seattle because they were concerned that he was becoming withdrawn and bored at his current school. He thrived there, excelling in all his classes. It was there where he was first exposed to computers. During his pivotal eighth grade year, the school acquired a Teletype Model 33 ASR terminal and secured a block of computer time on a General Electric (GE) computer for the students. This was a rare tool for schools to have access to at this time. Gates quickly became hooked on the promise and future of computer programming. It was also at Lakeside where he met Paul Allen, his future business partner. They became instant friends and bonded over their love of computers.

In 1970, at the age of fifteen and while still at Lakeside School, Gates and Allen developed a computer program that examined traffic patterns in their hometown of Seattle; they sold it to the city, earning $20,000 for their efforts. Soon after, Gates and Allen wanted to start their own company, but Gates's parents wanted him to finish high school and go to college, where they hoped he would become a lawyer.

Gates graduated from Lakeside in 1973. He scored 1590 out of 1600 on the college SAT test, something that young Gates would brag about when he met new people. He was accepted to Harvard University, and that fall he began his prelaw studies. However, he quickly found that he spent much more time in the computer lab and had no interest in the law. The future of Microsoft was on its historic course.

Defining the Problem

Personal computing was in its infancy in the early 1970s. Although computers had been developed and used by large corporations and governments for some time, they were too expensive and large to be used by any one person or organization without a lot of money. With the advent of the microprocessor, individual personal computers became affordable and small enough to interest more consumers. Early personal computers were often sold in electronic kits, usually to hobbyists and technicians. It was one of these very kits that Gates and Allen read about and became interested in, and which led to their founding Microsoft Corporation.

Designing the Solution

Around 1974, when Gates was still attending Harvard, Paul Allen showed Gates an article about the Altair 8800 minicomputer kit. They were both fascinated with what this computer could mean in the world of personal computing—they saw the real potential that computing had for the average person when most people did not. The Altair was made by MITS, a small company in Albuquerque, New Mexico. Gates and Allen contacted the company and told them that they were working on a **BASIC** software program that would run the Altair computer. In fact, they didn't have an Altair to work with or the code to run it—and they certainly had not written a software program to work with it! They asked the president of MITS, Ed Roberts, if the company was interested in someone developing such software. Roberts asked them for a demonstration.

Gates and Allen then spent the next two months frantically writing the software at Harvard's computer lab. Allen then went to Albuquerque to demonstrate the software they had developed, even though he and Gates had never tried it out on an Altair computer. It worked perfectly! Allen was hired at MITS, and Gates soon left Harvard to work with him. Their time at MITS was short-lived because in 1975, Gates and Allen formed a partnership they called Micro-Soft, a blend of "micro-computer" and "software." (They soon dropped the hyphen from the name.)

Including the word "software" in the company's name was not incidental. Microsoft wrote software in different formats for other computer companies and sold it on a licensing basis. Their first big score was to sell the MS-DOS operating system, which they purchased cheaply from another company, to IBM under a licensing agreement. IBM wanted to buy the source code, which would have given it the information to the operating system and greater control over how and when to use it. Gates refused, instead proposing that IBM pay a licensing fee for copies of the software sold with its computers. Doing this allowed Microsoft to license the software it called MS-DOS to any other PC manufacturer, should other computer companies clone the IBM PC, which they soon did.

A year after licensing the MS-DOS operating system to IBM, Microsoft's revenue reached $16 million. In 1985, Microsoft released the first version of Windows, its graphical user interface (GUI) that it adopted after seeing the way that Apple Computer was designing its interface, under the same licensing model. Windows was on nearly every PC in the developed world. Microsoft's profits skyrocketed.

Applying the Solution

In 1986, Microsoft went public. Gates held 45 percent of the company's shares and became an instant millionaire at age thirty-one. Over time, the company's stock became more valuable and split many times. In 1987, Gates became a billionaire when the stock went up yet again. Since then, Gates has been at or near the top of *Forbes*'s annual list of the top four hundred wealthiest people in America.

Gates was known for never feeling totally secure about the status of his company. He was always watching to see where the competition was. He was driven and competitive and expected the people around him to be the same. His difficult management style became legendary, and he would often challenge other employees' ideas to keep the creative process alive. Outside the company, Gates had a reputation as a ruthless competitor.

In 1989, Microsoft introduced Microsoft Office, which bundled office programs such as Microsoft Word and Excel into one system. These applications were not really compatible with OS/2, the older system that IBM partly owned. Microsoft's new version of Windows sold one hundred thousand copies in just two weeks, and OS/2 soon faded away. This meant that Microsoft had a basic monopoly on operating systems. Soon the Federal Trade Commission (FTC) began to investigate Microsoft for unfair marketing practices.

Microsoft faced several FTC and Justice Department investigations in the 1990s. Some charged that Microsoft made unfair deals with computer manufacturers who put the Windows operating system on their computers. Other charges stated that Microsoft forced computer manufacturers to sell the Internet Explorer browser if they wanted to sell the Windows operating system on their computers.

At one point, it looked as though Microsoft might be forced to break up its two main divisions: operating systems and software development. Microsoft defended itself and claimed that such restrictions were a threat to new ideas being developed. Eventually, Microsoft settled with the federal government and avoided the breakup. Gates continued to run the company and deal with the federal investigations through the 1990s. In 2000, Gates stepped down from Microsoft's day-to-day operations, and he and his wife founded the Bill & Melinda Gates Foundation.

The Impact of the Solution on Society

By shifting the value of the computer to the software, Microsoft commoditized computing and made it accessible for everyone. The importance of this statement cannot be exaggerated. Because of its approach to software computing—by setting software sales up as licenses—Microsoft Corporation helped lead to a PC being on every desk in every home and every office.

Microsoft built an operating system that let many others innovate, which in turn made PCs cheaper yet more valuable every year, which in turn meant more and more people could get access to them, in a continuous feedback loop. This innovation led to a period of great creativity.

It wasn't at all clear at the time Microsoft started that anyone could be successful in running a company that solely created software.

Gates's Personal and Philanthropic Life

In 1994, thirty-seven-year-old Gates married a twenty-eight-year-old Microsoft executive named Melinda French. She was bright and driven—a perfect match for Gates. In 1996, their first daughter was born. The couple went on to have two more children. Also in 1994, Gates's mother was diagnosed with breast cancer, and she died in June. Gates was devastated.

With Melinda's influence, Gates became interested in following his mother's example as a civic leader. In 1994, he and Melinda established the William H. Gates Foundation, which was dedicated to supporting education, world health, and investment in low-income communities. Thus began Gates's second successful career, this time in philanthropy.In 2000, the couple combined several family foundations to form the Bill & Melinda Gates Foundation. They started out by making a $28 billion contribution to set it up. The mission of the foundation is to "enhance healthcare and reduce extreme poverty globally, and in America, to expand educational opportunities and access to information technology." As examples, the foundation is responsible for donating over $1 billion to the Global Fund to Fight AIDS, Tuberculosis, and Malaria and has invested more than $250

Microsoft proved that it could be done, and how. Microsoft was a pioneer in software development and also in understanding how to sell and market computer products for a profit. Microsoft set the stage for the Internet revolution, which happened a few short years later.

In addition to being one of the most successful and richest businessmen in the world, Gates has also received many awards for his philanthropic work. For one, *Time* magazine named Gates one of the most influential people of the twentieth century. In 2011, Gates was ranked by *Forbes* magazine as the world's fifth most powerful person for his work with his foundation. Given that Gates is now just reaching his sixties, the world can hope and expect to benefit from his drive, determination, civic-mindedness, and intelligence for many more years.

million to create new small schools, reduce student-to-teacher ratios, and divide up large high schools in the United States.

Gates's involvement with the Bill & Melinda Gates Foundation occupied more and more of his time and interest, and in 2006, he announced he was retiring fully from Microsoft to devote all his energies to the foundation. His last full day at Microsoft was June 27, 2008.

Bill and Melinda Gates have helped many people with their foundation.

Timeline

1955
William Henry "Bill" Gates III born in Seattle, Washington

1968
Gates meets Paul Allen and is exposed to his first computer

1973
Graduates from Lakeside School and attends Harvard University to study law

1975
Gates drops out of Harvard and cofounds Microsoft Corporation with Paul Allen

1986
Microsoft goes public with an IPO of $21 per share

1994
Gates marries Melinda Ann French in Hawaii

2000
Gates steps down from the day-to-day operations of Microsoft; he and his wife found the Bill & Melinda Gates Foundation

2008
Gates retires from Microsoft Corporation

2014
Gates and his wife donate $50 million to the fight against Ebola

Inventor of the Computer Language Compiler

Grace Murray Hopper

1906–1992

As the computer began to evolve from a giant, complex machine that could only be operated by people who'd had extensive training in how to operate it to a more accessible object, a young American woman named Grace Murray Hopper devised a way of programming computers that was easier to understand. Her invention revolutionized the way people accessed the computer. It especially helped businesspeople, academics, and the military—and earned Hopper the nickname "Amazing Grace," mother of computing.

Grace Murray Hopper

A Curious Beginning

Hopper was born Grace Brewster Murray on December 9, 1906, and soon gained a reputation as a curious, scientifically minded child. By age seven, she was taking alarm clocks apart to see how they worked. Her father, Walter Fletcher Murray, was successful as an insurance broker despite having had both legs amputated. He passed on a spirit of determination to his three children; the oldest, Grace, learned from him that she could achieve whatever she set her mind to.

After graduating from Vassar College in 1928, Grace Murray went to Yale and earned her master's degree in mathematics in 1930. That year she married Vincent Hopper, an English teacher at New York School of Commerce, changing her name to Grace Murray Hopper. In 1934, she became the first Yale woman to earn a PhD in mathematics. Dr. Hopper returned to Vassar as a math teacher, becoming an associate professor in 1941.

Making a Contribution

When the United States entered World War II, Hopper was determined to contribute to the war effort. In December 1943, she was accepted by the US Naval Reserve and assigned to Harvard University. There, she joined a small team that used math to solve problems such as how to protect ships from mines. Her boss, computer pioneer Howard Aiken (1900–1973), greeted her with the words, "Where the hell have you been?" He set her to work on one of the world's earliest electromechanical computers, the Harvard Mark I. It was at this time that she wrote some of the first programs for the 51-foot (15.5-m) machine, as well as its five-hundred-page operating manual.

World War II brought tragedy to millions, including Hopper, whose husband was killed. After the war ended, she stayed on at Harvard to develop the improved Harvard Mark II and Mark III computers. During this time, she helped popularize the term "bug", meaning a programming error. Moths often flew inside the huge computers and stopped them from working. Removing the bug—or **debugging**—got the machine running again.

Defining the Problem

At this time, computers were used largely by universities and the military. Many people believed that no real market for business computers existed. Hopper thought differently. In 1949, she took a gamble with her promising career and joined a small company, Eckert-Mauchly Computer Corporation, founded by computer scientists John Mauchly (1907–1980) and J. Presper Eckert (1919–1995). There she helped to design the UNIVAC-1, the world's first large commercial electronic computer.

Complexity was one reason most people did not use early computers. Hopper realized computers would be employed in many more fields if they were easier to program and use, so she developed a compiler. She envisaged that people would write a program (the sequence of instructions for a computer to carry out) in meaningful symbols or English words. Her compiler would translate this program into raw, numeric instructions (machine code) that the computer could process. So the compiler was a kind of translator that helped computers and people to "understand" one another. Hopper worked for three years to convince her colleagues about the feasibility of her idea. She finally published the concept, called Flow-Matic, in 1952.

Designing the Solution

During the 1950s, Hopper took her ideas for compilers a step farther and helped to develop the first major computer programming language for business, called COBOL (COmmon Business Oriented Language). The language was designed with the consumer in mind. People using this language were likely to be involved in the business industry—managers, supervisors, and other businesspeople—and so Hopper and the others working on COBOL had to make programming easier to understand and execute. Like Flow-Matic, COBOL contained English-like elements such as verbs and clauses. This made it the most accessible and understandable programming language available at the time. Likewise, it became one of the first programs to be able to run on computers made by different manufacturers. It was widely popular with businesses and organizations, such as the US Department of Defense.

Applying the Solution

Hopper's invention transformed the way companies managed their business operations. COBOL enabled people to write computer programs for everyday business problems like preparing payrolls or billing clients using strings of simple English commands. Hopper joked that she helped to develop COBOL "because I couldn't balance my checkbook." Over time, COBOL became so useful that it remained a key computer program for businesses for decades.

In High Demand

From the end of World War II, Hopper remained in the Naval Reserve and combined her military work with her business career. In December 1966, she was obliged to retire from the navy after reaching the age of sixty. The navy soon realized it could not manage without her, so she was summoned back "just for six months" to sort out its computing problems. Almost twenty years later, she was still there. At age seventy-nine, she was the oldest serving officer and was given a grand retirement ceremony on the deck of the USS *Constitution*. By this time, she had been promoted to rear admiral—one of the most senior positions in the navy.

> "The most damaging phrase in the language is: 'We've always done it this way.'"
> —Grace Murray Hopper

The USS *Hopper*, pictured here in 2013, was named in Grace Murray Hopper's honor.

Although technically retired, Hopper immediately began a new career as a senior consultant to the computer maker Digital Equipment Corporation, touring the world to give lectures and spread her ideas. She drew a large, admiring audience wherever she went and continued this work until about eighteen months before she died on January 1, 1992.

The Impact of the Solution on Society

Grace Hopper is remembered as an original thinker: she had a clock in her office whose hands spun counterclockwise to challenge people to look at problems in new ways. Her thoughts and ideas helped form one of the most reliable, innovative programming languages. As of 2014—over fifty years after its inception—COBOL was still one of the most widely used programs in the financial sector.

Hopper received recognition for her achievements. Ironically, her first major award was to be named "Man of the Year" by the Data Processing Management Association in 1969. Other awards granted include the IEEE Emanuel R. Piore Award (1988) and the National Medal of Technology and Innovation (1990). In 1971, the Sperry

Corporation, for whom she worked, began an award in her name, which is still presented today to young people who excel in computer innovations. In 1973, she became the first person from the United States and the first woman to become a Distinguished Fellow of the British Computer Society. The navy named a ship for her—the USS *Hopper*—four years after her death, in 1996.

Grace Hopper was an inspiration to many: her achievements proved that women can be just as successful as men in scientific and technical fields, as well as in the military. Her legacy lives on to this day.

Timeline

1906
Grace Brewster Murray born in New York City

1930
Marries Vincent Hopper and becomes Grace Murray Hopper

1934
Hopper receives a Ph.D. from Yale

1949
Hopper helps design the UNIVAC-1

1952
Hopper develops and publishes her ideas for the first compiler

1950s
Hopper develops COBOL

1985
Hopper retires from the navy as a rear admiral

1992
Hopper dies

Inventors of the Apple I and Apple II Computers

Steve Jobs and Steve Wozniak

1955–2011 and 1950–

Since their beginnings in the 1970s, Apple Macintosh computers have become critical players in technological innovation. Today, Apple, Inc. is one of the world's most recognizable brands. Apple products such as the iPod, iPhone, and iPad tablet have transformed the way people interact with technology. However, it all started as a dream, one shared by two aspiring individuals: Steve Jobs and Steve Wozniak dreamt of making computers personal aspects of people's lives. It was a dream that would become reality and continuously influence the technology industry.

Steve Wozniak (*left*) and Steve Jobs (*right*) invented the Apple I computer in 1976.

Starting Out

Jobs and Wozniak grew up in the same town, Los Altos, California, though Wozniak was five years older. Stephen "Woz" Wozniak was born August 11, 1950, and developed his lifelong passion for electronics by emulating his father, who was an engineer. Another big influence was Tom Swift, a fictional teenage hero in Victor Appleton's adventure novels, who used science and creativity to solve problems and save the world. By fifth grade, Wozniak had built his first electronics and computer projects. He excelled at math and science at Homestead High School and went on to study electronics and computer science at the University of California at Berkeley. In 1971, he quit his studies and was hired as an electronics engineer by the Hewlett-Packard computer company.

Steven Paul Jobs was born in San Francisco, California on February 24, 1955, and was raised by adoptive parents in California. Like Wozniak, he showed an early interest in electronics. Jobs was lucky enough to befriend a neighbor who built electronic appliances from kits, so he understood how they worked. After attending Homestead High in Los Altos, Jobs attended Reed College in Portland, Oregon in 1972, but dropped out after only one semester. By 1974, he had been hired by the Atari Company to design computer games, but he left that job after one year to travel around India.

Innovation in the Seventies

The early 1970s were a remarkable time to be involved in electronics. In 1971, an engineer working at the Intel Electronics Corporation, Ted Hoff (1937–), invented a way of putting all the essential components of a computer onto one tiny silicon chip. This invention, known as the microprocessor or microchip, made possible such devices as pocket calculators and digital watches. Before this, the smallest computers were called minicomputers, but they were actually the size of a large washing machine—or bigger—and less powerful than the personal computers (PCs) in use today.

"It wasn't like we both thought it was going to go a long way—it was like, we'll both do it for fun, and even though we're going to lose some money probably, we'll just have been able to say we had a company."
—Steve Wozniak

In 1975, Ed Roberts, an American electronics enthusiast, used the new microchip technology to launch the world's first computer in kit form, the Altair 8800. Very primitive, it had to be programmed by flipping switches on its case, and it showed the results of its operations using rows of tiny red lights. It was more like a piece of laboratory equipment than a modern computer. Nevertheless, the Altair 8800 proved to be a big hit with electronics hobbyists, causing a particular sensation in one Palo Alto group calling themselves the Homebrew Computer Club. Among them were Steve Wozniak and his friend Steve Jobs.

Jobs and Wozniak first met at Hewlett-Packard, where Jobs had taken a summer job. By this time, Wozniak was already dabbling in the electronics business, making and selling small electronic gadgets called "blue boxes." Held near a telephone handset, a blue box would generate precise musical tones that could fool the exchange into allowing calls to be placed free. "Phone phreaking," as this was known, was popular in the early 1970s but was also illegal. Jobs and Wozniak sold the blue boxes for $150 each, although this "business" of theirs was run more for kicks and for undermining authority than to make money. For example, in the 1996 documentary *Triumph of the Nerds*, Wozniak gleefully recalls making a free call to the pope, while pretending to be Secretary of State Henry Kissinger.

Defining the Problem

Wozniak had often thought of building his own computer. Seeing the Altair at the Homebrew Club convinced him he could do much better. He was proud to be a **hacker** and was determined to turn his thoughts into a product. Wozniak worked for months on the project and showed off the results to his fellow club members in 1976. Like the Altair, the computer he made, the Apple I, was based on a microprocessor and built on a single circuit board. Unlike the Altair, it was programmed by entering commands on a typewriter-style keyboard, and it displayed results on an ordinary television set—it was altogether more "user-friendly." Members of the Homebrew Club were impressed, none more than Steve Jobs.

Designing the Solution

Wozniak has stated that he designed the Apple I just for the fun of doing it. However, when Jobs saw the machine, he saw the future. He persuaded Wozniak to go into business with him selling the Apple I in kit form. They needed money quickly, so Jobs sold his Volkswagen bus, Wozniak sold a valuable calculator, and together they raised $1,300 to start the business. On April 1, 1976, Wozniak and Jobs set up Apple Computer Corporation in the garage belonging to Jobs's parents. That year, they made and sold 175 kits priced at $666.66 each—far ahead of their expectations.

Wozniak was already working on a more advanced machine, the Apple II. It had more built-in memory, boasted color graphics, and could store programs using a cassette recorder. It could be programmed using the computer language BASIC—a series of English-like commands (such as GOTO, INPUT, and PRINT) that even a novice could quickly master. All these technical improvements were Wozniak's doing. However, the genius of the Apple II lay just as much in the way it was marketed—Steve Jobs's arena. Jobs realized that the machine needed to be packaged in a nice-looking plastic case, like a television or a stereo, and it needed to appeal to ordinary families, not just computer hobbyists.

Applying the Solution

When the Apple II was launched in April 1977, it cost $1,298—twice as much as the Apple I. In the next few years, Apple Computer sold more than fifty thousand of the machines. By the end of 1980, the little company Jobs and Wozniak formed in a garage had made its debut on the stock market, transforming its founders into multimillionaires. The Apple II stayed in production for a decade, and its success turned Apple into one of the world's biggest companies. Jobs and Wozniak were the toast of the computer world—but everything was about to change.

Leaving Apple

Success brought Steve Wozniak a private plane, but when he crashed it in February 1981, he thought hard about his life and decided to leave Apple for a while. With more time for his personal life, he married and organized music and technology festivals. In 1983, he

Inside Apple's Designs

Apple pays a great deal of attention not just to the internals of its products (how they work and what they do), but also to their external appearance. Designing a product to appeal to its potential users is an essential part of modern inventing and is known as **industrial design**.

Apple's iPod music player is widely regarded as an excellent example. With an appealing and sophisticated look, the original iPod has very few keys or switches to clutter its case, is easy to use, and has no lengthy instruction manual. Many people describe the design, created by Jonathan Ive (1967–), as "clean" and "timeless."

Industrial design helps to sell products by making them seem different from the competition. With electronic gadgets such as MP3 players and smartphones, products from different manufacturers tend to work in similar ways and perform similar functions or actions; consumers may struggle to tell them apart or choose between them. For such products, industrial design can make all the difference between success and failure. In Apple's case, its simplistic designs are part of what attracts so many customers to buy its products.

returned to the University of California at Berkeley to finish his degree, protecting his privacy by enrolling under the name Rocky "Raccoon" Clark. Later that year, he returned to Apple to help develop new products, but he left for good in 1985. He has since devoted much of his time and money to educational and charity projects and teaches electronics and computing to young children

Steve Jobs also said good-bye to Apple in the 1980s, but much more dramatically than his partner. He had recruited John Sculley, a senior executive from the Pepsi soft drink company, to help him manage Apple's spectacular success. Jobs and Sculley had very different ideas of the company they thought Apple should become, and Jobs was ousted in 1985 after a boardroom battle. Jobs later recalled, "What had been the focus of my entire adult life was gone, and it was devastating."

Jobs soon developed new interests. One was a company called NeXT, a designer of expensive computer workstations and software. Although technically advanced—Tim Berners-Lee used a NeXT computer to develop the World Wide Web—NeXT never achieved the success Jobs desired. His other project was Pixar, a graphics studio that developed computer technology for the film industry. From the mid-1990s onward, Pixar produced a series of spectacularly successful animated movies, including *Toy Story*, *A Bug's Life*, and *Monsters, Inc*., and made Jobs a billionaire.

Steve Job Returns

By this time, Apple was in deep trouble. The Macintosh was still using 1980s technology, and its archrivals, Microsoft and Intel, had joined forces to dominate the personal-computer business. Apple's board fired Sculley and hired other managers to halt the decline, but the situation grew steadily worse. In 1996, Steve Jobs agreed to return to Apple as an unpaid adviser; the following year, he was back in charge. Paid a salary of just one dollar per year, Jobs was listed in the *Guinness Book of World Records* as "The World's Lowest-Paid Chief Executive Officer."

Jobs had lost none of his marketing flair. In the 1970s, he had used his charisma to launch the Apple II as a "cool" product that every computer enthusiast should aspire to own. His amazing knack for selling products led one Apple engineer to suggest that Jobs generated a

Steve Jobs unveils the iPhone in September 2007

"reality distortion field (RDF)," a way of mesmerizing employees into accomplishing the impossible and charming customers into buying things they did not really need. In 1984, Jobs repeated that trick with Apple's Macintosh.

After returning to Apple in the 1990s, he worked the same magic with the iMac (1998), a redesigned version of the Macintosh; the iPod portable music and video player (2001); the online music store iTunes (2003); the revolutionary iPhone (2007); and the iPad (2010). Taking Apple back to its roots, with innovative products and attractive design, Jobs soon restored the company's vision—and its fortune. However, Jobs's influence would sadly end in 2011, when he resigned as CEO due to health problems. On October 5, 2011, Jobs passed away from complications of pancreatic cancer. His vision, enthusiasm, and insight for the company will always be remembered and uplifted.

The Impact of the Solution on Society

With the Apple I and Apple II, Steve Jobs and Steve Wozniak invented not only a pair of technically brilliant personal computers but also the concept of user-friendly personal computing. Until the Apple II went on sale in 1977, computing was just a hobby for electronics enthusiasts. When the Apple II became the computer of choice for small businesses in the late 1970s, the world's biggest computer company, IBM, was forced to launch its own personal computer, and it did in 1981. These actions resulted in most personal computers working the same way, running compatible software, and becoming easier to use. The personal-computer revolution was under way.

Jobs and Wozniak had envisioned this revolution many years earlier. As Jobs said later, "The thing that bound us together at Apple was the ability to make things that were going to change the world."

Apple products have always been known for their combination of technical innovation and appealing design—this is the legacy of Wozniak and Jobs. Jobs provided the vision; Wozniak (and his successors at Apple) made technical breakthroughs that enabled the vision to become a reality. The Apple story suggests that modern inventing involves marketing as much as innovation. Although neither technical brilliance nor marketing alone is enough to guarantee that an invention will succeed, together they often make a winning combination.

Timeline

1950
Stephen Wozniak born in Los Altos, California

1955
Steven Paul Jobs born in San Francisco, California

1971
Wozniak hired by Hewlett-Packard

1974
Jobs hired by the Atari Company

1976
Jobs and Wozniak found Apple Computer

1977
Wozniak and Jobs launch the Apple II

1981
Wozniak leaves Apple

1984
Apple releases the Macintosh

1985
Jobs forced to leave Apple

1985
Jobs founds NeXT

1996
Jobs returns to Apple

2000s
Apple introduces the iPod (2001), iPhone (2007), iPad (2010)

2011
Steve Jobs dies

Inventors of the Integrated Circuit

Jack Kilby and Robert Noyce

1923–2005 and 1927–1990

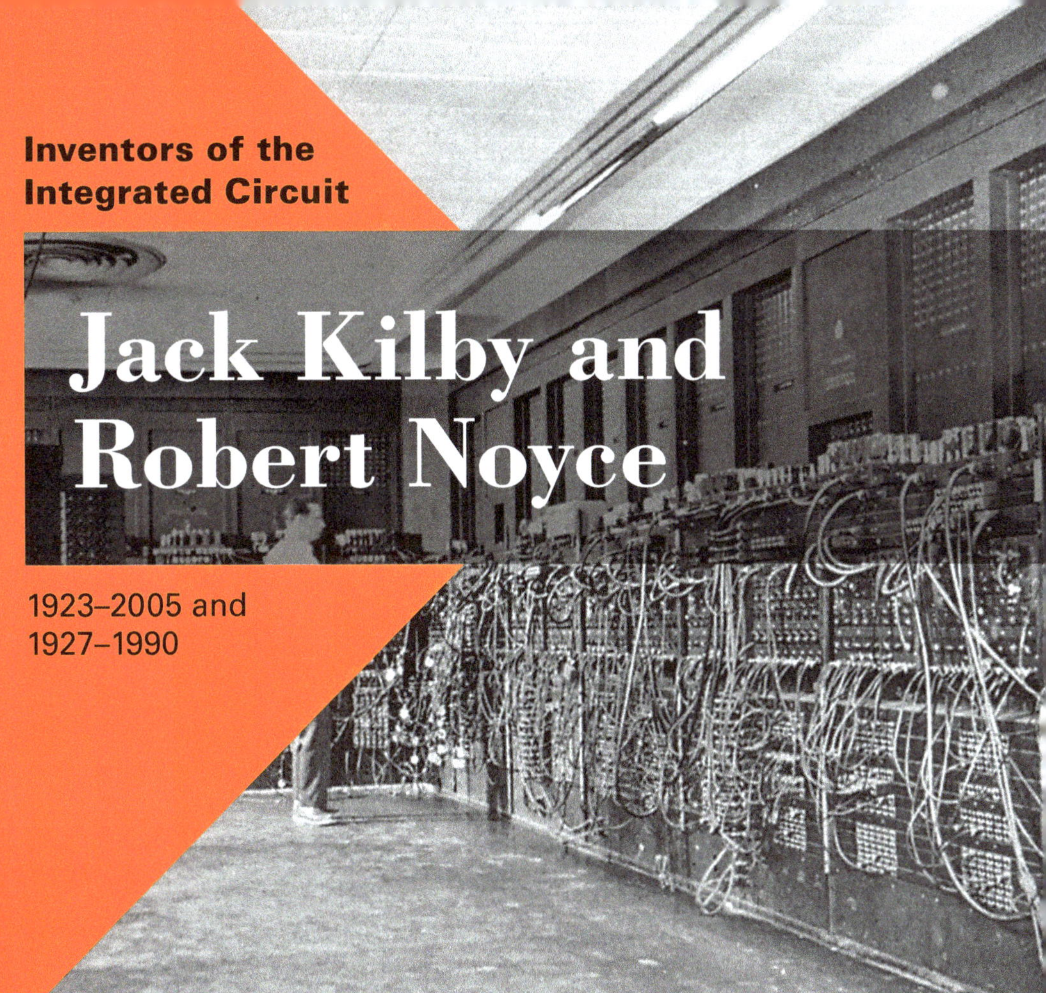

The first computers that were developed in the 1940s were massive, some as large as entire rooms. To operate them took skill and a working knowledge of thier many components. Today, however, computers can be as small as the face of a watch. All of this was made possible with the invention of the integrated circuit, a piece of complex electronics manufactured on a tiny chip of silicon. This mechanism was created in the late 1950s by an electrical engineer named Jack Kilby and improved upon and commercialized later by scientist and inventor Robert Noyce.

Jack Kilby in 1985

Robert Noyce in 1978

Beginnings

Jack St. Clair Kilby was born on November 8, 1923, in Jefferson City, Missouri. In 1927, his family moved to Kansas, where his father took the position of president of the Kansas Power Company. Kilby became interested in electricity as a boy when a huge ice storm knocked out power lines across Kansas and his father called on amateur radio operators to put out emergency messages. Kilby found the idea of sending invisible information through the air using electricity fascinating: "I first saw how radio—and by extension electronics—could really impact people's lives, keeping them informed and connected, giving them hope." Shortly afterward, he built his own radio transmitter–receiver.

After finishing high school, Kilby entered the University of Illinois in 1941. His studies were interrupted when he was called for military service in June 1943. During World War II, his background in radio led to his being deployed as a maintenance technician on military radio transmitters in India, Burma, and China. Later, he described his peaceful military duty as "a fascinating tourist experience." After the war, he returned to the university, graduating in 1947.

Robert Noyce, four years younger than Kilby, also came from the Midwest. The son of a preacher, he was born on December 12, 1927, in Grinnell, Iowa. Breezing through high school, he earned a reputation as an amazingly bright and well-rounded boy—a gifted physics student and a swimmer, diver, actor, choirboy, and musician. He was also something of a prankster. In the mid-1940s, having enrolled at Grinnell College, where he was majoring in physics, he stole a pig from a farmer so he and his friends could roast it in the dormitory. The farmer called the local sheriff and pressed charges; Noyce was thrown out of college for the semester. Noyce eventually graduated in 1949 and then moved to Massachusetts Institute of Technology (MIT) to earn his doctorate.

Electricity Versus Electronics

Both Noyce and Kilby studied electronics, still a new field in the mid-twentieth century. Electricity involves supplying power to appliances using quite large electric currents (steady flows of electricity); electronics involves controlling appliances using tiny currents. An electric circuit can make a lamp glow, but an electronic circuit can sense when it is dark and switch the lamp on automatically. Electronics is "intelligent electricity" with switches that turn on and off under different conditions.

"Don't be encumbered by history: go off and do something wonderful."
—Robert Noyce

The first electronic switches were called vacuum tubes, and they could either switch electric currents on and off or amplify them (make them bigger). Vacuum tubes were invented in 1906 by US radio pioneer Lee de Forest (1873–1961) and were used in early radio sets to amplify incoming signals so people could hear programs more easily. Vacuum tubes revolutionized radio, but by World War II they were also finding their way into early electronic computers. The worst problem with vacuum tubes was their size: each one was about as big as an adult's thumb. They also glowed like little lamps, got very hot, and used immense amounts of power. A useful computer needed thousands of these tubes. ENIAC (Electronic Numerical Integrator and Calculator), a remarkable computer built in 1946, used around eighteen thousand vacuum tubes, which resulted in a machine 100 feet (30 m) long and 8 feet (2.4 m) high, weighing 60,000 pounds (27,215 kg).

Defining the Problem

Early computer pioneers realized that vacuum tubes were limiting the complexity of the machines they could build. What was needed was a better, smaller, more reliable electronic switch. Three US physicists—John Bardeen (1908–1991), Walter Brattain (1902–1987), and William Shockley (1910–1989)—produced such a switch when they invented the transistor at Bell Laboratories in 1947. Transistors shrank electronic switches from the size of a thumb to the size of a fingernail—but thousands of them still took up space, and much time was needed to wire them together.

Designing the Solution

After graduating from the University of Illinois with his degree in electronic engineering, Jack Kilby took a job with Centralab, a small electronics firm in Milwaukee, Wisconsin. For three years, he worked during the day and studied for a master's degree in electronics in the evenings. At Centralab from 1947 to 1958, he designed circuits for radios, television sets, and hearing aids. Centralab also paid for him to go to Bell Laboratories so he could learn about the new transistor technology. He remembered later: "I felt the transistor pointed the way to the future, and I wanted to be there." Early in 1958, he decided to leave Centralab to work for a bigger manufacturer that would let him specialize in what became known as microelectronics: making tiny electronic components.

In May, Kilby joined Dallas-based Texas Instruments. As he was a new employee, he had no vacation that year; over the summer, he had the laboratory virtually to himself. He started looking into an idea that an English scientist, Geoff Dummer, had suggested several years earlier: electronic components might possibly be made from layers of semiconductors—materials such as silicon and germanium that allow electricity to flow only when impurities are added to them. By July, Kilby was writing in his notebook that he thought all the different parts of a circuit could be made from a chip of the same semiconductor. He called this the **monolithic principle**. About a month later, on September 12, 1958, Kilby produced the first monolithic integrated circuit, a tiny electronic circuit made using a single chip of germanium. Shortly afterward, Texas Instruments patented the idea.

Applying the Solution

Five years before, in the summer of 1953, Robert Noyce had completed his doctorate at MIT and gone to work for Philco, an electronics company in Philadelphia. At Grinnell College, his physics teacher had shown him transistors made by Bardeen, Brattain, and Shockley at Bell Laboratories—and that memory had stayed with him. In 1956, William Shockley set up his own firm, Shockley Semiconductor, in Palo Alto, California. When word got around that Shockley was hiring bright young physicists, Noyce moved his family to California. Noyce was so confident Shockley would give him a job that he bought a house in Palo Alto before he had even had his interview. As expected, Noyce got the job. Over the next year or so, he enjoyed his work, knowing that the research he was doing was at the very cutting edge of electronics. However, this satisfaction did not last.

Shockley, a brilliant physicist, was a poor manager, and his employees soon became discontented. In 1958, eight of his best researchers—including Noyce—quit to set up their own firm, Fairchild Semiconductor. Although the original plan had been to devise a better transistor, Noyce ended up inventing something like Kilby's integrated circuit. He also developed a way of using chemistry and photography to make these tiny integrated circuits on pieces of silicon. Known as the planar process, Noyce's invention allowed hundreds, thousands, and eventually millions of transistors to be placed onto a single silicon chip.

Just like Kilby, Noyce decided to patent his version of the integrated circuit—which raised an immediate problem: Who had actually invented the device? Kilby had made the first attempt and had successfully created all the parts of a circuit on a chip. However, he had wired his components in the traditional way. Noyce had gone a step further, creating both the components and the connections between them using the same process. Noyce's circuit was truly integrated, and his patent was more detailed. Kilby's patent application was denied and Noyce's was granted in April 1961. This provoked a furious response from Texas Instruments, which started a legal battle with Fairchild that continued until 1969. In the end, the companies agreed to share the rights to the invention, and Jack Kilby and Robert Noyce have been considered joint inventors of the technology ever since.

Integrated Circuits

An electronic circuit board is a bit like a miniature town. Instead of homes, schools, factories, and stores, a circuit is packed with small components called transistors, capacitors, resistors, and diodes. Connections run between these components just as streets connect buildings in a town. The electronic traffic that runs down these streets allows the circuit to do a particular job.

Until the late 1950s, all circuits were built from many different components pushed into holes in a circuit board with wires or metal interconnections linking them together. Then Kilby and Noyce

invented the integrated circuit and everything changed. An integrated circuit does exactly the same job as a traditional circuit but it is made in a different way. As Noyce later recalled, "I was trying to solve a production problem; I wasn't trying to make an integrated circuit." Instead of having components pushed into holes, the components and the connections between them (the "buildings" and the "streets") are made from the same material, called a semiconductor.

Metals such as gold and copper let electric currents flow through them easily and are known as conductors; other materials, like wood and plastic, do not let electricity flow so well and are called insulators. Still other materials, including the chemical elements silicon and germanium, are semiconductors: they are normally insulators but turn into conductors if impurities are added to them. This process is called doping.

Silicon can be doped in two ways. One process creates a kind of silicon with slightly too many electrons, known as n-type; another produces silicon with slightly too few electrons and is called p-type. Using a process that involves a mixture of photography and chemistry, electronics engineers can take a thin piece of silicon (called a wafer) and create a patchwork of n-type and p-type areas all across its surface. When electricity flows through the wafer, these different areas work together like microscopic transistors, diodes, and other components. All the components and the connections between them are built up (integrated) from a single piece of silicon—and so the whole thing is called an integrated circuit.

Integrated circuits are made up of many microchips.

Slow and Steady Success

Many thought the integrated circuit had no future. Some felt the new technology was too complex and expensive and would not turn a profit. Others believed electronic components were best made the traditional way. The adoption of integrated circuits was slow until two breakthroughs in the 1960s. First, the US Air Force used the technology in Minuteman guided missiles. These missiles were paramount to defending the country during the Cold War. Second, NASA used integrated circuits in the Apollo moon-landing space rockets. These impressive demonstrations of miniaturization, power, and reliability led computer manufacturers to embrace the technology.

Another revolution happened soon afterward. In July 1968, Noyce and his colleague Gordon Moore (1927–) left Fairchild to set up their own company, Integrated Electronics—Intel for short. In 1971, building on Noyce's earlier work, a brilliant engineer at Intel, Ted Hoff (1937–), found a way to pack all the essential components of a computer into a single chip or microprocessor. This revolutionized the electronics and computer industry and made Noyce, Moore, and their colleagues at Intel some of the richest people in the world.

The Impact of the Solution on Society

Integrated circuits have since revolutionized computing. In 1946, ENIAC, with its eighteen thousand vacuum tube switches, was truly the state of the art. That kind of computing power was available only to universities and the military. In 1965, Gordon Moore discovered that the number of transistors engineers could pack onto a chip had doubled every year or two since the 1950s, and he predicted that the same remarkable progress would continue. This idea, which became known as Moore's law, spurred engineers on to even greater achievements.

When Intel invented the microprocessor in 1971, it became possible to squeeze two thousand transistor switches onto a chip of silicon the size of a small fingernail. Today, more than one billion transistors will fit into the same amount of space. The underlying trend is for a doubling of transistors every eighteen months or so—however, in 2014, it became more difficult to cram more transistors into the chip. As the *Economist* reported, "No exponential trend can carry on forever, and some think the end of the silicon transistor may now be in sight." Nevertheless, the impact of the integrated circuit has been truly phenomenal.

End of the Era

Inventing the integrated circuit at age thirty-five was undoubtedly Jack Kilby's finest hour. He was employed by Texas Instruments until 1970, when he left to work as a freelance inventor. Much of his work involved finding uses for the technology he had developed. One of the best-known applications is the electronic pocket calculator, which Kilby helped to invent in the mid-1960s. Using his knowledge of electronics, he also experimented with solar cells: devices that use semiconductors such as silicon to turn sunlight into electricity. Kilby's important contribution to electronics was recognized with many honors. In 1982, he was inducted into the National Inventors Hall of Fame; in 2000 he was awarded the **Nobel Prize** in Physics. Kilby died at the age of eighty-two on June 20, 2005.

Although Robert Noyce died fifteen years before Jack Kilby, his legacy is arguably greater—largely because of his role in setting up Intel. Noyce remained modest about his wealth, yet he enjoyed its pleasures: he built a large house, bought expensive sports cars, learned to scuba dive, and flew paragliders and vintage airplanes. With Intel's success ensured, he became the company's chairman in 1974 and left the day-to-day management to others. Robert Noyce was inducted into the National Inventors Hall of Fame in 1983. He died of heart failure at age sixty-two on June 3, 1990.

Lasting Legacies

Jack Kilby and Robert Noyce came from similar backgrounds and followed similar paths to success. They started out as small-town boys, gained a good college education, then went to work for electronics companies where they made great discoveries. Many other twentieth-century electronics pioneers came from similarly modest backgrounds. Noyce had a theory about this: "In a small town, when something breaks down, you don't wait around for a new part, because it's not coming. You make it yourself."

Whereas Jack Kilby made his mark entirely in technical areas, Robert Noyce also revolutionized how electronics companies were managed. At both Fairchild Semiconductor and Intel, he introduced an informal, West Coast working style in which everyone has a similar-size cubicle, no one has a reserved parking space, and a corporation becomes a community to which people devote their lives. His impact was not just on the products that an electronics company developed but on the way it developed them. The culture of Silicon Valley (the area of California where many electronics companies operate) owes much to his influence; Noyce was nicknamed "mayor of Silicon Valley" for this reason. Would the integrated circuit have happened if Jack Kilby and Robert Noyce had not developed it? Almost certainly: as Kilby acknowledged, the Englishman Geoff Dummer had already had the idea some time before; and Kilby and Noyce arrived at the same invention by different routes. With growing pressure to develop better computers, someone else would surely have done the same thing. The microelectronics revolution would have happened eventually, but thanks to Kilby and Noyce, the world enjoyed its benefits sooner rather than later.

As part of Intel's informal culture, the founders decreed that there would be no reserved parking spaces in the company's vast parking lot. "If you come late," Noyce was often heard to say, "you just have to park in the back forty."

Timeline

1923
Jack St. Clair Kilby born in Jefferson City, Missouri

1927
Robert Noyce born in Grinnell, Iowa

1947
Kilby graduates from the University of Illinois

1953
Noyce earns his doctorate from MIT

1958
Kilby designs an integrated circuit; Noyce and colleagues start Fairchild Semiconductor

1961
Noyce patents his integrated circuit

mid-1960s
Kilby invents the electronic pocket calculator

1968
Noyce leaves Fairchild to found Intel

1970
Kilby leaves Texas Instruments

1982
Kilby inducted into the National Inventors Hall of Fame

1983
Noyce inducted into the National Inventors Hall of Fame

1990
Noyce dies

2000
Kilby awarded the Nobel Prize in Physics

2005
Kilby dies

Inventor of Antivirus Software

John McAfee

1946–

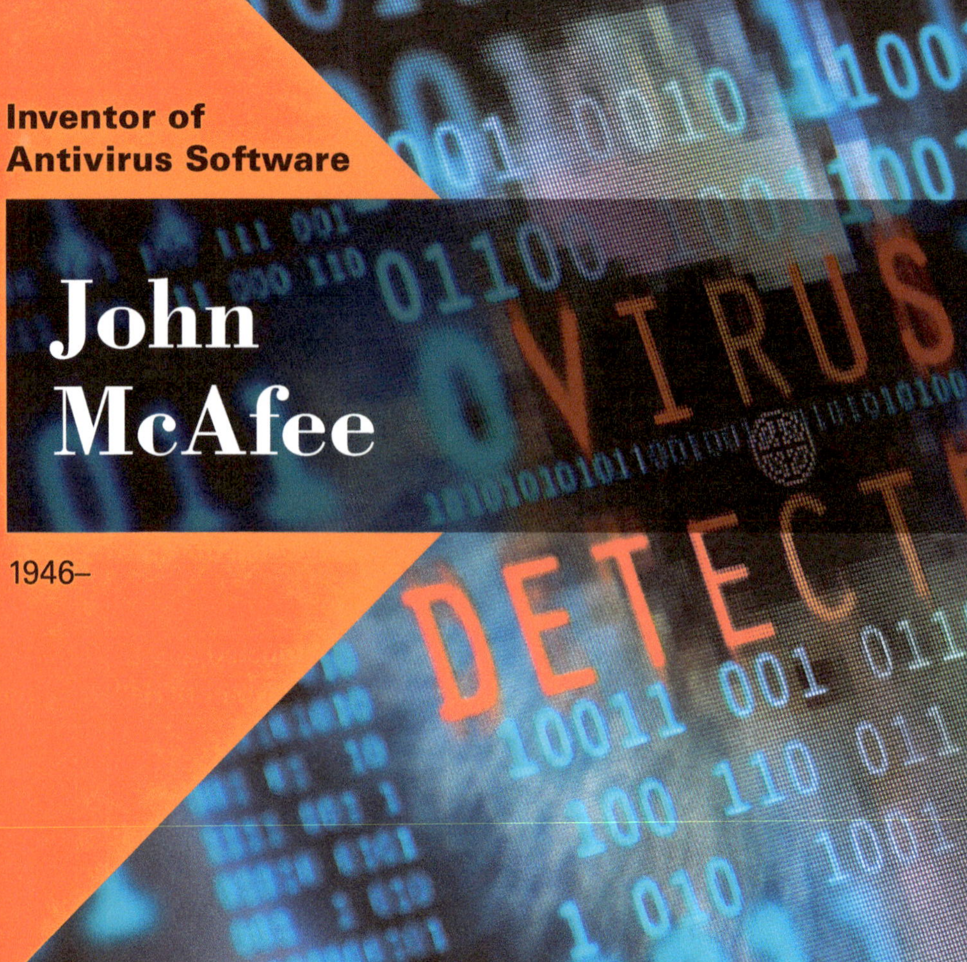

Inventions have many positives, and they open doors to new experiences and opportunities. They can, however, generate problems that are sometimes difficult to resolve. In the 1980s, the personal computer came into being. In its basic form, it was difficult to see how a problem could arise from this machine. Evolution of the machine, however, brought problems in the form of hackers and **viruses** to the computer market. An attempt to combat these problems was invented in the mid-1980s by a man named John McAfee. He invented the first **antivirus software** and changed the way computers armed themselves against outside threats.

Birth of an Inventor

John McAfee in August 2013

Born in England in September 1946, John McAfee has lived most of his life in the United States. He grew up in Salem, Virginia, and earned his bachelor of science degree in mathematics at Roanoke College. McAfee has always loved learning and believes colleges offer their students a unique opportunity; he later recalled, "You have the umbrella that isolates you from reality; that is, the world outside. The college campus is the most magical place on Earth because you get to create a reality of your own making."

After graduating from Roanoke in 1967, McAfee studied mathematics at Virginia Tech until 1970. He then moved to Silicon Valley, an affluent part of California centered on Stanford University, where many electronics and computer companies are located. By his own account, he held at least a dozen different jobs during this time, most of which involved developing computer hardware or software.

Defining the Problem

During the mid-1980s, McAfee was working as a computer software designer for the Lockheed Corporation when he stumbled on a virus of a different kind. He later remembered, "It was an accident, like anything else in life." His computer became infected with what was named the Brain virus, a malevolent program originally written by two students in Pakistan that could erase files from a computer's hard drive.

Although McAfee knew enough about computers to solve the problem and deactivate the virus, he doubted that most users would cope so well. This inspired his big idea. In 1987, he left Lockheed to set up his own business, helping companies and individuals address their computer security problems. Taking to the road in a Winnebago mobile home, he traveled around the country, driving to people's homes and businesses and fixing their computer problems.

Working Antivirus Software

Computer viruses take their name from biological viruses, which infect organisms by working their way in from the outside world. Similarly, a computer virus seeks to gain access to a computer's hard drive, infect one or more of the programs on it, and destroy either the programs, the data, or both. At the same time, it tries to spread itself to other people's computers. As late as the mid-1990s, viruses spread almost entirely on **floppy disks**. In the contemporary world, almost all viruses come from the Internet. Typically, they arrive in e-mail attachments, but they can also be hidden among random Internet traffic.

An antivirus program is a piece of software that runs permanently in the background of an individual's computer system, checking for viruses and trying to isolate them when they appear. Programs such as this use several different defensive techniques, the most common being to keep a list of "signatures" of all the known viruses. The signature is a set of unique identifiers for each virus. It might include, for example, a certain e-mail header that the virus always uses or other important signs, such as telltale changes that the virus makes to a user's hard drive. Antivirus software regularly scans all the files and programs on a computer, looking for anything that might match its list of virus signatures.

The major drawback of this method is that it can detect only known viruses—new viruses that have a different signature are likely to go undetected. Antivirus software can get around this with generic scanning, in which it searches for suspicious files and **quarantines** them as a precaution. Also, just as the Internet has made distributing viruses easier, it has also made fighting them easier: most antivirus programs now automatically download updates. While the antivirus writers struggle to stay up to date, hackers are continually developing new ways of breaching systems. The two camps are in a constant battle to outsmart each other.

Designing the Solution

McAfee soon realized he could automate some of this work. He wrote VirusScan, the world's first antivirus computer software. When permanently loaded onto a computer, VirusScan could detect and remove known viruses. Writing the program was one stroke of genius; the way McAfee sold the program was another. Instead of retailing his software in a store, McAfee used a technique called shareware. He gave away a version of the program as a free trial but charged corporations for licenses and technical support if they continued to use it.

Applying the Solution

By the end of the 1980s, antivirus software had made John McAfee rich and famous. In addition to his best-selling program, he also wrote a book on the subject: *Computer Viruses, Worms, Data Diddlers, Killer Programs, and Other Threats to Your System* (1989). McAfee realized that fighting computer viruses was a lucrative business. He decided to found an organization called the Computer Virus Industry Association (CVIA) and make himself the chairman. Journalists soon began to approach McAfee for his views on the latest computer security threats and what he thought users should do about them.

In early 1992, the press found out about an apparently dangerous new virus, nicknamed "Michelangelo." According to computer security experts, it was programmed to lie dormant in machines until March 6, 1992, when it would suddenly "wake up" and destroy the hard drives in which it was concealed. Several weeks before this date, the media approached McAfee and the CVIA for their views. McAfee apparently told the journalists that the virus could infect from "fifty thousand to five million machines." Only the latter figure was reported, however, causing panic to spread throughout the computer industry.

When March 6, 1992 dawned, few computers were affected by the virus. Many people turned on McAfee, accusing him of making an inaccurate prediction—a charge he denied. Others made a more serious accusation, suggesting he had deliberately fueled the Michelangelo scare to help sell his company's software. The critics

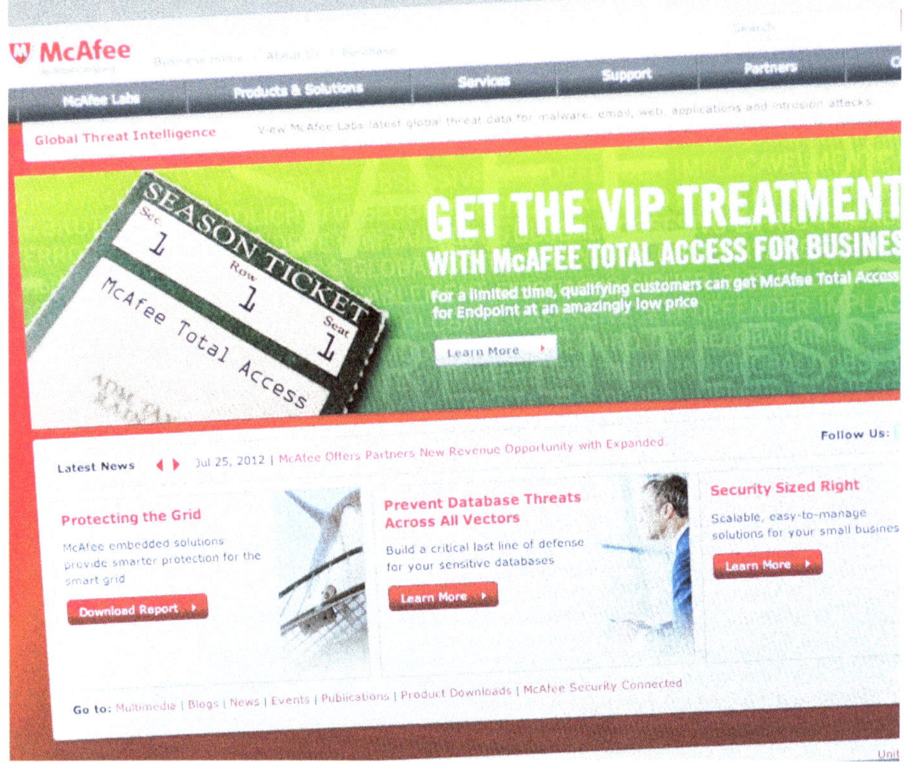

McAfee, Inc. remains one of the top antivirus software companies today.

believed their suspicions were confirmed when McAfee Associates reported a huge increase in business in 1992. McAfee vigorously denied this charge as well.

The following year, McAfee took his company public, raising more than $50 million. Reports differ about what happened next. Some say McAfee chose to retire with a large payment for his services; others claim he was asked to leave because of a continuing backlash over the Michelangelo virus. Whatever the case, John McAfee resigned from McAfee Associates in 1994 as a very rich man.

Pioneer of Instant Messaging

John McAfee was only forty-eight years old in 1994. He moved from Silicon Valley to Colorado, where he bought 400 acres (162 hectares) of forest, on which he built a home. Around this time, Tim Berners-Lee's World Wide Web was beginning to catch on, and the world's first easy-to-use web browser had just been launched. Many people were talking about the Internet—and John McAfee saw a new opportunity.

His idea was to create an online (Internet-based) community called PowWow. The plan was to give away a sophisticated instant messaging (IM) chat program. McAfee imagined people would use it to make new friends online and set up interest groups or "tribes." Some of the features now used in Internet chat programs such as the MSN, America Online (AOL), and Yahoo! instant messaging programs began in PowWow. This kind of "social software" has since become one of the most popular uses of the Internet, perhaps best known on Snapchat, Ello, and Facebook. However, in 1994, social software was still a relatively unexplored field. Several years ahead of its time, PowWow brought together many different capabilities that could not then be done with a single program.

Between 1994 and 2000, approximately eight million people joined PowWow and set up tribes. Unfortunately for McAfee, however, the Internet at that time was almost entirely dominated by large service providers such as Yahoo! and AOL. These firms had no intention of allowing a rival service to prosper at the expense of their own chat programs and online communities. As the competition increased, PowWow struggled for survival among the bigger firms. McAfee eventually sold his stake in the company for an undisclosed sum; PowWow went out of business in January 2001. McAfee failed to find the same degree of success with PowWow that he had achieved with his security software. Nevertheless, he had demonstrated an important concept, and other companies soon rushed to exploit the idea.

Still a very rich man, McAfee decided to try a different approach. In 2000, he became a major investor in Zone Labs, a computer security firm. At the same time, his name continued to sell antivirus software for his old company, McAfee Associates, briefly renamed Network Solutions, and now doing business as McAfee, Inc.

The Impact of the Solution on Society

John McAfee can be credited with creating not just the world's first antivirus program but the entire antivirus software industry. Cynics might claim that this industry has exaggerated the problem of computer viruses for its own benefit. However, McAfee did not invent the computer virus—and if he had not developed antivirus software, someone else would surely have done so. Most people who use antivirus software still place their faith in it and believe it to be essential for keeping the problem in check. By the early twenty-first century, antivirus software was a multibillion-dollar industry. The company McAfee founded continues to be a dominant provider of antivirus software, and while it has met competition, it is among the world's top computer security organizations. As of 2015, McAfee himself was living in a small town in Tennessee working on a new project in technology, Future Tense Central. Likewise, he planned a technology conference featuring key people in tech development, such a Nolan Bushnell and Brock Pierce.

John McAfee's influences on the computer technology industry extend to more than just antivirus software. His decision to distribute his VirusScan program free so he could later profit from business sales and service was an early model for how businesses can make money in the Internet age, and while his innovative PowWow program may have failed, it helped to begin a type of online chat community that is now the core of the Internet for many people.

Timeline

1946
John McAfee born in England

1967
McAfee graduates from Roanoke College

1970
McAfee moves to Silicon Valley, California

1987
McAfee sets up his own computer-security business

1993
McAfee Associates goes public

1994
McAfee resigns from McAfee Associates; creates PowWow

2000
McAfee becomes a major investor in Zone Labs

2015
McAfee starts new venture in security software, Future Tense Central

Inventor of eBay

Pierre Omidyar

1967–

As the popularity of the Internet and the World Wide Web grew throughout the 1990s, they inspired other innovations. One of the most revolutionary inventions was developed in 1995 by a man named Pierre Omidyar. Omidyar envisioned a new way for people to buy and sell products online, in an auction-style setup. The invention, eBay, soon became one of the most accessible and successful products developed in a new digital age.

Born Abroad

Pierre Omidyar was born in Paris, France in 1967 to a French-Iranian family. In the early 1970s, his father, a physician, moved the family to the United States when he accepted a residency at Johns Hopkins

Pierre Omidyar gives a talk during the annual Clinton Global Initiative conference in 2010.

University Medical Center in Baltimore, Maryland. Later, the Omidyar family moved to Washington, DC.

Omidyar first learned about computers a few years later, in middle school, when he started using a Radio Shack TRS-80 microcomputer (an early version of today's home computers). He taught himself programming using the language BASIC. At the age of fourteen, he wrote a program to catalog the books in his school library.

His fascination with computers continued into high school and, eventually, he earned a degree in computer science at Tufts University in Medford, Massachusetts. After graduating in 1988, Omidyar went to work for Claris, a company owned by Apple Computer that developed programs to run on Apple's machines. He left Claris in 1994 and worked at two small Internet start-up companies, Ink Development (later named eShop) and General Magic.

Defining the Problem

For years, many people thought eBay was invented when Omidyar was at dinner with Pam Wesley, his fiancée. An avid collector of PEZ candy dispensers, Wesley began to tell Omidyar about the trouble she was having finding new items for her collection. Omidyar thought it was just the sort of problem the Internet might be able to solve. The real story, however, is not as glamorous: Omidyar simply wanted a way to turn a hobby into a business.

Designing the Solution

Launched on September 4, 1995, eBay was initially called Auction Web. The first item sold was a broken laser pointer, which went for $14.

Originally, Auction Web was hosted on Omidyar's own web space. Soon afterward, he moved the site to its own **domain**. This created an immediate problem: professional websites cost money to run. So Omidyar decided to charge sellers between 25 cents and $2 to list their items. At this time, nearly everything on the World Wide Web was free, and the idea of charging for anything was controversial. Even so, to Omidyar's surprise, the site became extremely popular, and he was soon making enough money to leave his job and work on Auction Web full time.

Applying the Solution

In 1996, Omidyar hired Jeffrey Skoll, a Stanford business graduate, to help expand his business. By the following year, Auction Web was hosting hundreds of thousands of auctions every day. During 1997, they renamed the business eBay.com (a shortened version of Echo Bay, the name that Omidyar had originally wanted for the company) and the spectacular growth continued. By 1998, the firm had a million registered users and hired a professional CEO, Margaret Whitman, from the toy firm Hasbro. Whitman continued the spectacular run of success, and by the end of 1998, Pierre Omidyar's personal stake in the firm was valued at around $3 billion: eBay had made him one of the first Internet billionaires.

Life Following eBay

Wealth was not, in itself, that interesting to Omidyar. With eBay established, he decided to step back from the company and use his newfound fortune to invest in other projects. Many people view eBay simply as an online auction room, but to Omidyar it was something much more interesting. He saw it as an example of "social software"—a way of using computers to bring people together to achieve positive outcomes for humankind.

In 1998, Omidyar married Wesley, and in 2004, the couple set up the Omidyar Network, their personal foundation. It is designed to finance social projects so that "more and more people discover their own power to make good things happen." The organizations they support include Creative Commons (which encourages people to publish books, photographs, music, and other creative works freely on the Internet), SourceForge (which helps programmers to develop freely available or "open source" software), and Meetup (a website that enables people to locate and meet others who share their interests). In 2013, Omidyar and his wife launched their flagship journalism organization, First Look Media. The company "seeks to improve society through journalist and technology." Both Omidyar and his wife promised to "invest $250 million to create new forms of independent journalism," according to *Forbes*. They have also invested at least $115 million in the Humanity United foundation, which "funds eighty-five antislavery nonprofits as well as projects in five countries." Pierre and Pam Omidyar have announced their intention to give away 99 percent of their personal wealth by the year 2020.

Famous Investors in Society

Many successful inventors eventually become **philanthropists**. Pierre Omidyar, Microsoft's founders Bill Gates and Paul Allen, and Larry Ellison (founder of the computer software company ORACLE) are some of the world's richest people; they are also some of its greatest philanthropists. Although there are tax advantages to giving away personal wealth, most philanthropists genuinely believe in using their money to help humankind. For example, the Bill & Melinda Gates Foundation uses its $40 billion endowment to help tackle global diseases and improve education.

Philanthropy is by no means a modern phenomenon. American steel magnate Andrew Carnegie (1835–1919) spent the last years of his life donating money to help found public libraries and establish Carnegie Mellon University. Many other universities also have been founded by philanthropists. Stanford University in California was established when railroad baron Leland Stanford (1824–1893) donated land and money to commemorate his recently deceased son. The area known as Silicon Valley in California, where many computer and electronics firms are based, grew up from a science park built on Stanford University's land. Many graduates of Stanford

The Impact of the Solution on Society

By many measures, eBay has been one of the Internet's most spectacular successes. With more than one hundred million registered users around the world, selling tens of thousands of different types of goods, it has rapidly become one of the world's most important trading places. Yet its impact has been even greater. Websites such as eBay, Yahoo!, and Google have helped to create what is sometimes called a "virtuous spiral." By encouraging many more people to go online, they have created an immense growth in Internet use, benefited from that growth, and, in turn, created even more growth in the Internet.

One of the more surprising aspects of eBay is how readily strangers will trust one another when they exchange even very expensive goods. Although auction fraud is not uncommon, most people still have a positive experience when they buy and sell online.

have gone on to make fortunes of their own by working in computer start-up companies. Some of these individuals have, in turn, become prominent philanthropists: eBay's first president, Jeff Skoll, was a Stanford business graduate and, like Pierre Omidyar, has set up his own charitable foundation. A close and continuing link between successful invention and philanthropy can often be found as each helps the other to thrive.

Silicon Valley is a popular area for computer companies' headquarters.

The idea that the Internet can strengthen human communities is a very powerful one, and Pierre and Pam Omidyar are now using their Omidyar Network to prove the point.

In one sense, Pierre Omidyar is a very modern inventor: only since the 1990s have inventors had the opportunity to use the Internet to develop new ideas. In another sense, he is a classic inventor who saw a gap in the marketplace and developed a product to fill it. The Internet's growth and eBay's growth have served to help each other—making Omidyar one of the first great inventors of the Internet age.

Timeline

1967
Pierre Omidyar born in Paris, France

1988
Omidyar graduates from Tufts University

1994
Omidyar begins work at Ink Development and General Magic

1995
Omidyar launches his website, Auction Web

1997
Auction Web is renamed eBay.com

1998
Omidyar's personal stake in eBay is valued at $3 billion

2004
Omidyar establishes the Omidyar Network

2013
Pierre Omidyar and his wife, Pam, launch First Look Media

Inventor of the Compact Disc

James T. Russell

1931–

Technology has changed in many ways over the decades. Entire industries have been transformed. Two such examples are the music and film industries. They were changed forever by the invention of the compact disc (CD) and the digital video disk (DVD). The man behind these inventions is James Russell. He was the first person to envision these products, and over time, greater organizations and the public took notice. Before long, these inventions would change the way people interacted with not just music and film but also television, video games, and digital files.

Birth of the Inventor

James Russell was born in Bremerton, Washington in 1931. He became interested in science and engineering at a young age—at the age of six, he built his own model of a navy ship. He was also a tremendous fan of classical music from childhood; this aspect would prove important to the history of his invention. He attended Reed College in Portland, Oregon, and graduated with a degree in physics in 1953.

James Russell in 2005

After graduating, Russell found a job as a physicist with General Electric, which had contracted with the federal government to manage the Hanford nuclear plant, located in southern Washington. At Hanford, Russell became interested in creating new tools, designing, among other implements, a welder that used a beam of electrons.

Defining the Problem

The Hanford plant was built during World War II to provide plutonium and uranium for atomic and nuclear weapons. Because of its military importance and the sensitivity of the work, Hanford was located in a remote area of Washington State. Russell, who was living in nearby Richland, discovered that no radio stations in the area played classical music. To listen to the classical music he loved, Russell relied on his phonograph.

However, the phonograph was unsatisfactory on many levels; for one, records were played with heavy steel needles, which quickly wore out the records. Russell began exploring ways to make his records last longer, including using phonograph needles made of cactus spines. The spines did not ruin the records, and they produced a better sound than the steel needles, but cactus needles wore out quickly and had to be sharpened constantly.

Russell decided that the music industry needed a record-and-needle combination that would never wear out because the record and needle would never actually come into contact with each other. He thought the needle might be replaced with a laser.

Designing the Solution

Russell did not act on his idea until 1965, when Battelle Memorial Institute, a nonprofit research organization, took over management of Hanford from General Electric. Russell and the other staff members at Hanford became Battelle's employees, a change Russell anticipated would allow him to research his interest in lasers. He soon persuaded his new employers to let him develop his idea of creating an optical system that could be used to record and play music.

By 1970, Russell had created the first compact disc. As with today's CDs, the music was digitized into a code etched onto the disc using a laser. A laser was also used later to read the code, which was translated into musical sounds by a player. Russell's disc, however, differed in many ways from modern CDs; for example, the disc was about 12 inches (30 cm) in diameter.

Reinventing Video

As Russell developed his audio system, he realized that if music could be digitized, so could video. Russell was optimistic about the potential of this idea. "The vision I had in mind was of television programs on little plastic records," he later said. "The networks, instead of putting programs on television, would print records. And if you wanted to watch your favorite programs you'd get them in the mail and put in the disk whenever you want."

Much to Russell's frustration, Battelle lost interest in developing his optical-storage ideas. A venture capitalist, Eli Jacobs, did show interest, however. Jacobs founded Digital Recording Corporation in 1971 to fund Russell's research into video disks. Russell created a working video recorder/player that was unveiled in 1974.

While working on the video recorder, Russell filed for a patent on a technique that is still used in compact discs. The technique allows a player to read data on discs in the correct order, a task called **synchronization**.

Numbers of Music

One of Russell's insights in developing the CD was the idea that something as flowing and amorphous as music could be represented digitally. He later recalled the reactions he received: "'Music into numbers? Come on now, Russell.' When I first proposed it, it was not believed that you could digitize sound."

Previously, only analog recording had been used. In analog recording, a microphone picked up sound using a diaphragm that vibrated: the vibration was etched directly onto a record. When a record was played, a needle physically replicated that vibration, which was then translated back into sound. The problem was that the needle would eventually wear away the record's grooves. This led to degradation in quality and prompted Russell to develop a system in which a laser "needle" would never actually touch the recording medium.

Such a system would rely on digital recording. The concept of recording music digitally struck Russell's contemporaries as unorthodox but proved easy to accomplish. When a song or a sound is recorded on CD, the recorder samples the sound many times. In modern CDs, more than forty-four thousand samples are taken for each second of sound recorded.

Each sample is assigned a numeric value, which is then burned onto the CD with a laser. When the CD is played, a laser reads the numeric value of the many samples, and the CD player translates those values back into sound. Because so many samples are taken, the result is an extremely accurate sound recording that, if played properly, is never degraded by being scratched with a needle.

Applying the Solution

The video player Russell developed attracted a good deal of interest. Representatives from several large electronics companies, including Sony Corporation and Royal Philips Electronics, were sent to evaluate the technology. At the time, companies like Philips had developed a laser optical disc that, unlike Russell's technology, which digitized audio and video to make it clearer, relied on analog recordings and was often of poor quality.

None of the companies that had been interested in Russell's technology proved willing to partner with Digital Recording, however, and the firm began to flounder. In 1985, Digital Recording went bankrupt. Its intellectual property—including Russell's patents—was acquired by a Toronto firm, Optical Recording Corporation. The company offered the inventor a two-year contract as a consultant, which he accepted, moving to Toronto.

The Impact of the Solution on Society

By then, compact discs were becoming a big business. Sony and Philips had introduced the first commercially available CDs in 1982. Although sales were initially slow, the improved sound quality of digitized music quickly gained the attention of audiophiles. In addition, compact discs began to interest the computer industry because they could store a great deal of information in a relatively small space.

"Although an inventor's life is often frustrating, particularly as one tries to convince others of the feasibility of an idea, it is also enormously exciting and in the end satisfying to create a useful device, a new technology, and even, on occasion, a new industry."
—James Russell

Sony and Philips significantly modified Russell's original design. Their CDs were much smaller and were in many ways more sophisticated. Nonetheless, the underlying technology was extremely similar to Russell's ideas, which had been protected by more than two dozen patents.

Russell's patents had been controlled by his previous employers, who had not gone to much trouble to enforce them, most likely because the compact disc was still a very new technology. As the compact disc became increasingly popular, however, Optical Recording decided to take far more aggressive action to protect Russell's patents.

In 1986, Optical Recording notified every other company in the compact disc industry of the patents it controlled, offering them the chance to negotiate a settlement in lieu of taking the case to court. Two years later, the company reached its first major licensing agreement with Sony; agreements with Philips and many other large companies followed.

One holdout was the entertainment giant Time Warner, which was manufacturing music CDs using Russell's synchronization technique. Optical Recording took Time Warner to court, and in June 1992, a federal jury found that Time Warner had violated Optical Recording's patent. Time Warner, which had by then manufactured 450 million compact discs, was ordered to pay Optical Recording $30 million.

Looking to the Future

Russell, however, received none of that money. His two-year contract with Optical Recording had expired before the company reached its first licensing agreement, and he had moved back to Washington.

Today, the popularity of CDs has waned, as new video- and music-streaming services, such as Netflix, grow.

Russell worked as a consultant, establishing a company called Ioptics in Bellevue, Washington, in 1991. Ioptics focused on developing computer memory systems that used light; such systems would store more data and be faster than conventional memory storage. The low cost of traditional memory and production problems at Ioptics combined to drive the firm out of business in 1999. For his achievements with the compact disc, however, Russell did win recognition. In 2005, the Puget Sound Engineering Council chose him as Industry Engineer of the Year. Today, Russell lives in Bellevue, where he works as an optics consultant.

Russell's patents expired in the early 1990s, a few years before the introduction of the DVD made his idea of television programs on records a reality. The CD had largely replaced the vinyl record as the dominant format for music and the floppy disk as the dominant format for software. The DVD would do the same, largely replacing videotapes. Today, however, DVDs and CDs are being faced with new threats, particularly digital video and music streaming. The two may not disappear completely from society, as many people still rely on both for entertainment purposes, but their popularity is diminishing due to such new, more accessible technological innovations.

Timeline

1931
James Russell born in Bremerton, Washington

1953
Russell graduates from Reed College with a degree in physics

1965
Russell begins working on a digital recording and playback system

1971
Russell creates a video recorder

1982
CDs become commercial available

1991
Russell founds Ioptics

1999
Ioptics closes; Russell works as a consultant in the field of optics

Inventor of the Linux Operating System

Linus Torvalds

1969–

Since the dawn of the Internet in the 1990s, many new and fascinating changes have occurred in society. More and more people have invested time and money in their own computers, and as a result, they have needed new, reliable tools by which to operate them. Some users have even contributed directly to the evolution of the computer and more advanced technology, such as smartphones and tablets. Perhaps one of the most popular operating systems to which many people have contributed is Linux (pronounced Linn-ucks), a free rival to the popular Microsoft Windows operating system. Linux is named for Linus Torvalds, the Finnish computer programmer who created it in 1991.

Early Years of the Inventor

Linus Torvalds at the Millennium Technology Prize award ceremony in Helsinki, Finland, in 2012

Linus Benedict Torvalds was born in Helsinki, Finland on December 28, 1969, and was named for Linus Pauling (1901–1994), an American chemist and Nobel Prize winner. His father, Nils, works in broadcasting; his mother, Mikke, is a journalist. In his 2001 autobiography, *Just for Fun*, Torvalds describes himself as having been "an ugly child," "a beaverish runt," and "a nerd—before being a nerd was considered to be a good thing."

During the early 1980s, he became interested in computers and acquired a Commodore VIC-20, an inexpensive and quite basic home computer largely designed for playing games. Later, he bought a more powerful machine and started to tinker with its operating system. Torvalds had no idea that his growing interest in operating systems would dramatically change not only his life but also the world of computing.

Defining the Problem

In 1988, Torvalds began studying at the University of Helsinki for a degree in computer science. It would take him eight years to complete, not graduating until 1996. He began normally enough, doing much of his college work using the UNIX operating system, which had become popular in universities in the 1970s. Then, in 1990, he bought an IBM personal computer (PC) that ran DOS (disk operating system), a different operating system that had been developed by Microsoft. Torvalds thought DOS was greatly inferior to UNIX and wondered if a UNIX-like program could be made to work on the IBM PC instead.

Designing the Solution

He was not the first to try this. An American academic, Andrew Tanenbaum, had already written Minix, a UNIX-like operating system for the IBM PC. After inspecting Minix closely and suggesting modifications to the system (which were not taken under consideration), Torvalds instead decided to create his own program. Throughout the spring and summer of 1991, he shut himself inside his bedroom in his mother's apartment and worked on the code—the list of instructions that make up a computer program—around the clock. According to his mother, there was nothing very strange about this behavior: "Just give Linus a spare closet with a good computer in it and feed him some dry pasta, and he'll be perfectly happy."

"What really matters is that people are very involved in generating the best technology they can."
—Linus Torvalds

In August of that year, he posted an announcement on a computer bulletin board: "I'm doing a (free) operating system (just a hobby, won't be big and professional ...)." After he wrote the kernel, or core, of his operating system, he made it freely available on the Internet, allowing anyone to download it or submit improvements. Torvalds originally called his system Freax, combining three words that seemed to sum up what he was attempting: Free, Freak, and UNIX. A coworker later changed the name to Linux, and after mulling it over, Torvalds agreed to adopt the name for his operating system.

Applying the Solution

As the 1990s progressed, Linux became an astonishing phenomenon. Tens of thousands of programmers joined the effort to develop it into an operating system that could challenge Windows, the operating system that Microsoft produced after DOS. Like the conductor of some enormous worldwide orchestra, Linus Torvalds took time off from working on his college degree to direct the effort. Some of the programmers helped to build up the Linux kernel; others developed or modified application programs to make them compatible with Linux. However, Torvalds always remained in charge in a friendly but determined way. As he said to one programmer about a proposed change to Linux in 1996, "If you still don't like it, that's OK: that's why I'm boss. I simply know better than you do."

The Impact of the Solution on Society

The success of Linux earned Torvalds widespread admiration in the computing world. Under his guidance, Linux had become not just an affordable operating system but one that had other advantages, too. For instance, it could be quicker and more powerful than Windows, more robust, and less likely to crash when something went wrong. It was also more secure against viruses and similar threats. Advantages like these made Linux increasingly attractive to computer users.

By January 2000, Linux was such a trustworthy piece of software that IBM, the world's biggest computer company, announced that it was going to make all its computers run on the system. In the years that followed, more and more computers and devices

Reinventing Inventions

Linus Torvalds has helped to popularize a whole new approach to inventing. Several aspects make his Linux program different from an ordinary invention. Most obviously, it is a free product—free in the sense that it is usually given away. This is possible because the programmers who work on Linux want to be part of a community effort that helps people; they do not especially want to make money. Unlike most inventions, Linux is free from copyright and patent restrictions; thus it can spread and evolve much more quickly than an invention bound by legalities.

Linux is also different in being the product of thousands of inventive minds. Although Linus Torvalds started this effort alone, the large majority of the Linux code has since been written by others. Because so many people are involved in the project, Linux has developed much more quickly than would have been possible had Torvalds worked alone. This kind of "group inventing" is possible largely because of the Internet, which allows people to chat, e-mail, and exchange their creations almost instantly. The huge success of Linux has inspired many others to try this method of creation; Wikipedia, for example, is a free Internet encyclopedia comprising several million articles written by tens of thousands of enthusiasts. People can share their ideas through Linux's company website, linux.com, and its foundation's website, linuxfoundation.com.

used Linux. According to the website linuxfoundation.com, Linux "is everywhere." Today it "powers 98 percent of the world's supercomputers, most of the servers powering the Internet, the majority of financial trades worldwide, and tens of millions of Android mobile phones and consumer devices." According to *Forbes*, "it has nearly 21 percent market share." It is a system that seems here to stay.

Linus Torvalds speaks at the LinuxCon Europe convention in 2014

Linux Meets Conflict

In 1991, Linux had just one user, Linus Torvalds; a decade later, millions had switched to the system—largely because it was free. Linux is free in two senses: it is available for free download and it is also free from copyright, so people can share and modify it. Programs like this are known as open source: the original software, or source code, is freely available to others to use as they wish.

Open-source programs can be very attractive to users. However, big companies that sell software for a fee, such as Microsoft, have sensed a growing threat from the huge army of volunteer programmers who are developing software this way. In 2003, one such company, Santa Cruz Operation (SCO), sued Linux because it claimed that parts of Linux were closely based on UNIX, which SCO owned at the time. IBM, Linux's lead partner, also became involved. During the course of the court process, other issues arose between SCO and other IBM companies, but at the center was the Linux debacle. Since Torvalds and his developers built their system from huge amounts of donated program code, it was difficult—perhaps impossible—for them to confirm that none of their code had been copied from software developed by other companies. In 2006, the case seemed to have reached an end, concluding that SCO's evidence was not strong enough. However, in 2013, the company reared its head again, bringing unresolved issues to light when it asked a Utah judge to reopen the case. He did. The case is still in development.

The Future for Torvalds

Today, Linus Torvalds still assists Linux. He is one of the **Linux Foundation** fellows and the main authority on what code goes into the Linux kernel. He has also participated in many talks about the fate of his program. According to a talk at LinuxCon in October 2014, the Linux company is still doing well and continues to grow. A new update of Linux is released every "two to three months." Torvalds is responsible for checking that all of the various modifications to the program have not caused major changes to the system's ability to operate. The changes are relatively minor and are monitored and approved, a procedure that differed in earlier years of Linux's existence. Torvalds estimates that there are "around ten thousand patches with every release from more than a thousand people." Each update brings new material and an improved edition of the successful operating system. With all its success, it seems Linux will continue to grow and thrive for many more years.

Timeline

1969
Linus Torvalds born in Helsinki, Finland

1991
Torvalds completes the kernel of Linux

1996
Torvalds finishes his computer science degree from the University of Helsinki

1997
Torvalds begins to work at Transmeta Corporation

2000
IBM announces that all its computers will run on Linux

2003
Torvalds begins work at the Open Source Development Labs

2014
Torvalds speaks at LinuxCon about the future of Linux

Founder of Wikipedia

Jimmy Wales

1966–

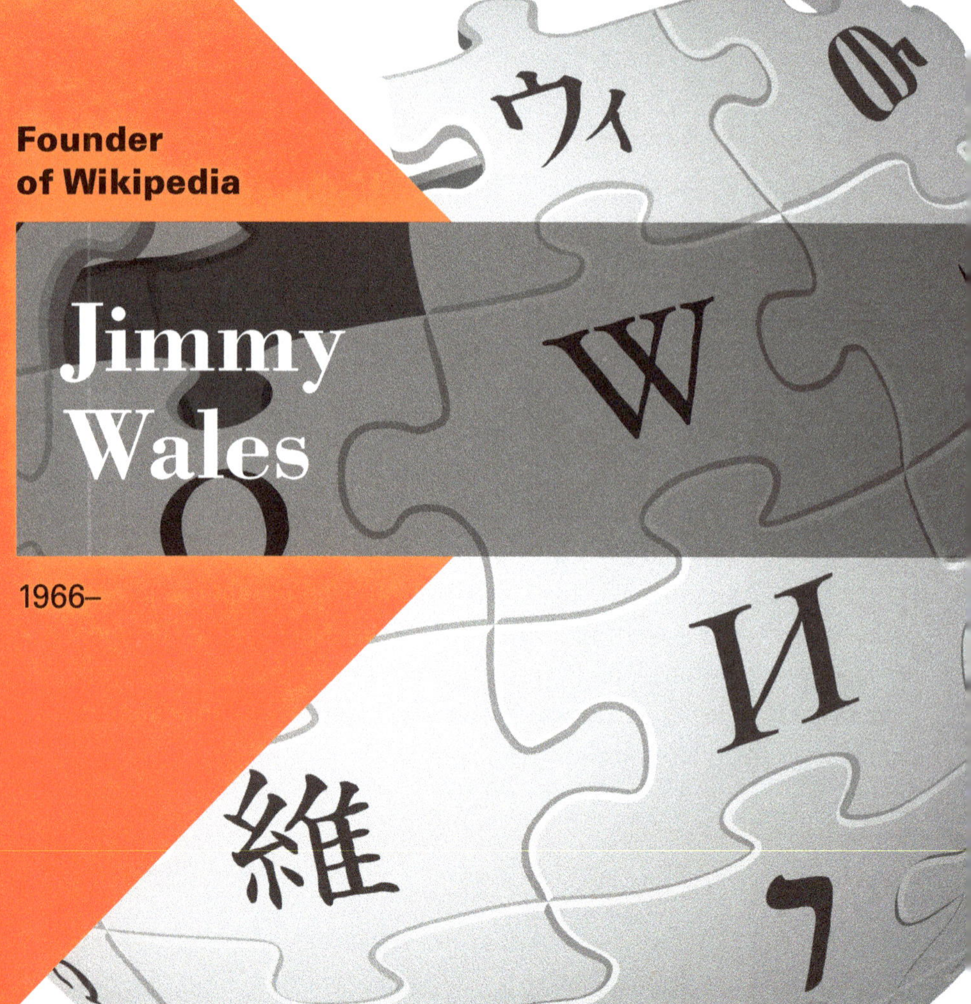

When you look up something on the Internet today, what are the first websites that appear? Many times, near the top of the results list is Wikipedia. This website is one of the most comprehensive online encyclopedias. Its inventor, Jimmy Wales, created it to fill a void in the online reference market. Since its beginning, it has challenged the way people research online, and sometimes it has caused problems. Nonetheless, it is a fascinating collaboration between people around the world and offers more than 16 million articles in more than 270 languages, all provided without ads or fees. It has profoundly affected global access to reliable and verifiable knowledge, and perhaps most important—as Wikipedia itself claims—it has made knowledge on virtually any topic a person could want to research, accessible in a few clicks.

Growing Up

Jimmy Wales, founder of Wikipedia, in June 2014

Jimmy Wales was born August 7, 1966, in Huntsville, Alabama to a hardworking middle-class family. His father worked as a grocery store manager. His mother, Doris, and grandmother, Erma, ran the House of Learning, a one-room schoolhouse built on the Montessori model of education. Montessori places emphasis on independence, freedom within limits, and respect for a child's natural educational and social development. Children learned in a self-directed manner, and Wales remembers spending much of his time poring over encyclopedias and World Book encyclopedias. Wales and his three siblings attended this school through the eighth grade. He has said that "education was always a passion in my household," and he attributes his self-directed upbringing with his ability to think creatively. After eighth grade, Wales attended Randolph School, a university-preparatory school in Huntsville. He graduated at sixteen.

In 1986, Wales graduated with a degree in finance from Auburn University. He then began but did not finish a doctoral program in finance at Indiana University. After leaving the doctorate program, Wales took a job at a trading firm in Chicago. During his spare time, he wrote code, played virtual role-playing games, and studied the growth and maturity of the Internet as it was happening. He watched the Internet from the sidelines, until 1996, when he decided to leave financial trading and become an Internet entrepreneur. He used money he had earned speculating on interest-rate changes to fund his first website start-up, called Bomis. It was financially successful; in fact, he used the money he made from it to fund Wikipedia in its early days.

Defining the Problem

Wales went on to found several website start-ups, most of which later failed or ran their course. He had always been interested in the Internet and its potential to serve the masses in a democratic way. His career in finance turned out to be short-lived, and he instead followed his passion to develop an idea that eventually became known as Wikipedia. His goal was no less than to provide free and unfettered knowledge worldwide.

In March 2000, meeting a long-time desire to provide free information to everyone worldwide through the Internet, Wales and some colleagues launched Nupedia, an open-content site that was moderated by its users. Nupedia was the direct predecessor to Wikipedia, but its content-approval process was much more cumbersome as it did not use the live **wiki**-based way of making changes. Instead, articles that were submitted to Nupedia had to go through a seven-step approval process before they would be posted.

Criticisms of Wikipedia

Wikipedia has not been without its detractors and bumps in the road. There have been several important and legitimate criticisms of Wikipedia. Two of the main ones are:

Accuracy and credibility of its articles
This was a more common concern during its first years, as people worried that the articles were inaccurate or not authoritative. Over time, the peer editing process and the responsibility that Wikipedia's writers and editors shoulder to get it right have created a rigorous editorial procedure. Articles are still sometimes vandalized, and bad or misleading information does leak out, but most people feel that the peer review process works in the long run to provide high-quality content.

Lack of the diversity of contributors and the bias that follows
As mentioned on page 124, the editors of Wikipedia are overwhelmingly male, young, highly educated, and from the Western world. When one population of people overwhelmingly contributes to anything, its preferences, culture, and biases tend to play out there. Wales and the foundation say that Wikipedia is making an effort to reach out to more women, older people, experts in the arts and humanities, and less-represented geographic areas such

Designing the Solution

In 2001, Wales and colleague Larry Sanger adopted the existing "wiki" content-management system software and called his site Wikipedia. Nupedia and Wikipedia coexisted for a short time, but Wikipedia attracted much more traffic and user participation, at least in part because the wiki model worked well for immediate, time-sensitive editing. The site is collaborative in nature. Hundreds of thousands of users worldwide write and edit its entries, and anyone can edit an entry or dispute a fact found on the site.

It's much easier to submit and edit articles using the wiki system, but some people, including Larry Sanger, thought that the traditional peer review that Nupedia used provided higher quality and a better degree of accuracy to the content. Wales sided with the wiki model at

as South America, South Asia, and the Arab world. As examples, it has launched partnerships on US college campuses to fill in some of these gaps, including recruiting humanities professors to assign students to write fully sourced articles for the site. It's also opening an office in India to provide relevant content there.

In almost every case, the foundation has been very upfront about Wikipedia's own limitations and has worked to overcome them.

Today, Jimmy Wales advocates for his company and foundation all around the world.

least in part because he understood that its ease of use would attract more users. The collaborative editing model would prove to be a hurdle to credibility that Wikipedia would have to overcome in time.

Applying the Solution

Almost immediately after its inception in 2001, Wikipedia rapidly grew in size and popularity. As Wikipedia's public profile grew, Wales became its promoter and spokesman in the media. He also went on the road speaking at universities and colleges about the value of open, transparent, free information and explained how Wikipedia was serving that need.

Wikipedia says its mission is one of spreading human knowledge worldwide, and it does so without ads or fees. It's written and edited by hundreds of thousands of users worldwide. Wales founded the nonprofit Wikimedia Foundation, which has overseen the development of Wikipedia since 2003. The internal operations of the site—server support, for example—are managed by around two hundred employees that staff the Wikimedia Foundation's office in San Francisco, California.

In order to ensure high accuracy and quality, volunteers filter through posts to identify questionable or unsourced information (when you add articles, you are expected to add inline citations that source your information). They can fix or flag information—by adding or requesting sources where there are none—and editors are generally discouraged from outright deleting information unless it is clearly a hoax or is vandalism.

The education of the average Wikipedia user is higher than the general population; 69 percent of Internet users with at least a college degree use the site. It is most popular with younger Internet users: 62 percent of those under thirty use Wikipedia, compared with 33 percent of Internet users age sixty-five and older. The editors of Wikipedia are 87 percent male and are an average of twenty-six years old, both of which Wales acknowledged as areas of concern. By comparison, the average age of a visitor to the site is thirty-six, with roughly equal numbers of men and women. One of Wikipedia's more recent goals is to work to provide a diversity of voices to the site.

The site currently contains more than 3.5 million articles written in English, and more than a million articles have been created in French and German. The encyclopedia receives more than 408 million unique visits a month, according to comScore Inc., a company that monitors Internet traffic.

The Impact of the Solution on Society

How has Wikipedia changed the way people use the web? It's profound when you consider that the answers to most questions are just a click away anywhere there's Internet access. Information that was once found only in authoritative textbooks or taught by teachers is now open to everyone, anywhere.

Although the accuracy of the information on Wikipedia has been met with skepticism over the years, many teachers now see it as a great place for students at least to start the research process. Instead of Wikipedia being a threat to their role, many educators see it as an indispensable companion.

In 2014, Wikipedia was ranked as the fifth most visited website worldwide, behind such sites as Google, Amazon, Facebook, and YouTube. From such success, it's clear that the idea that Wales created in 2003 has been a huge success.

Wales's Awards and Accolades

Because of his work creating and developing Wikipedia, Wales has received several major awards and honorary degrees from institutions. In 2006, he was named one of *Time* magazine's "100 Most Influential People." The World Economic Forum recognized Wales as one of the Young Global Leaders of 2007. This award acknowledges the top 250 young leaders in the world for their professional accomplishments, their commitment to society, and their potential to contribute to shaping the future of the world.

Other honors include the 2008 Global Brand Icon of the Year Award, the 2009 Nokia Foundation annual award, the Leonardo European Corporate Learning Award, the Pioneer Award in 2011, and the Gottlieb Duttweiler Prize. He was also ranked twelfth by *Forbes* on its list of "the Web Celebs 25."

Today, Wales continues to serve on the Wikimedia Foundation board and speak worldwide about Wikipedia.

Timeline

1966
Jimmy Donal "Jimbo" Wales born in Huntsville, Alabama

1983
Wales graduates from the Randolph School, a university-preparatory school in Huntsville, at age sixteen

1986
Wales graduates with a degree in finance from Auburn University

2000
Wales launches Nupedia

2001
Wales adopts the existing "wiki" model and launches the Wikipedia website

2006
Wales named one of *Time* magazine's "100 Most Influential People"

2007
Wales recognized as one of the Young Global Leaders by the World Economic Forum

Cofounder of Facebook

Mark Zuckerberg

1984–

With the advent of the Internet and the World Wide Web came new opportunities for people around the world to connect on levels like never before. Interacting with the World Wide Web created a global community where people could share ideas, ambitions, and perspectives. In the early 1990s, people took to online chat rooms and instant messenger systems to meet others with similar interests. However, as more and more people started to use the Internet, a need for a new type of social outlet arose. There were many attempts before an overwhelmingly popular answer arrived. In 2004, then-Harvard student Mark Zuckerberg developed "thefacebook," an interactive social media website for college students. Over time, it evolved into one of the world's most successful online social sites. Until Facebook, "social media" in the sense it's used today did not exist. The number of Facebook users worldwide reached a total of one billion in 2012. Zuckerberg's contribution to online social media is monumental, and Facebook, as it's known today, has made its mark on technological history.

Mark Zuckerberg influenced a social network revolution in the early 2000s with the introduction of Facebook.

A Natural Talent

Mark Elliot Zuckerberg was born May 14, 1984, in White Plains, New York, to Edward Zuckerberg, a dentist, and Karen Kempner, a psychiatrist. He was the only boy in a family with four children. He and his sisters grew up in Dobbs Ferry, New York, a small town about ten miles (16 km) north of New York City.

Zuckerberg began experimenting with computers and writing communications tools and games in middle school, when his father taught and encouraged him. His parents were very supportive of his fascination with computers and helped him in his endeavors. When he quickly grew past his father's computer knowledge, his parents hired a private tutor, specifically trained in computer programming, to meet with Zuckerberg once a week for personal computer/programming lessons. That tutor said he had a hard time keeping up with Zuckerberg's intellect and natural knack for programming.

Zuckerberg initially attended Ardsley High School, where he excelled in the classics, such as Latin and Greek. He transferred to Phillips Exeter Academy, an exclusive preparatory school in New Hampshire, his junior year, where he won prizes in math, astronomy, physics, and classical studies. His interest in computers did not diminish, however. He took a graduate course in computer programming at Mercy College near his home while still in high school. During this time, he built many usable software programs, including one in BASIC he called "ZuckNet" that allowed all the computers between the house and his father's dental office to communicate with each other. It was a primitive version of the first instant messaging program.

During his high school years, under the company he called Intelligent Media Group, he built a music player called the Synapse Media Player that used machine learning to teach itself the user's listening habits. It was essentially an early version of the program called Pandora and even received a rating of 3 out of 5 from *PC Magazine*. Several companies—including AOL and Microsoft—wanted to buy the software and hire Zuckerberg before he graduated from high school, but he declined.

By all accounts, Zuckerberg wasn't the typical "computer geek," in that he became captain of his prep school fencing team and earned a classics diploma in high school. In fact, he was often known by friends for quoting lines from epic Greek poems such as *The Iliad*.

He entered Harvard College in 2002, studying psychology and computer science, and his blossoming reputation for being the programming "go-to guy" grew. He created a program called CourseMatch, which helped students choose classes based on what other students in their areas of study had chosen and liked. He also created a program called Facemash, which compared pictures of two students on campus and allowed users to vote on which one was more attractive. Although this program became popular with the student body, the university later shut it down after it was judged inappropriate. The next idea he developed, collaborating with friends, became what we know today as Facebook.

Defining the Problem

When Zuckerberg and his two friends, Dustin Moskovitz and Eduardo Saverin, developed the Harvard-only social networking website, originally called "thefacebook," they did so to enable students to connect with each other, create their own profiles, upload photos, and socialize online. Before this time, computer networks hadn't been used in this way, at least not successfully so. There was no Instagram, no Twitter, no LinkedIn, no Snapchat. Although there had been attempts to create socializing websites, including such sites as Classmates.com (users could search for old classmates but not create profiles), SixDegrees.com, and Friendster.com, none of these had the right mixture of features and philosophy that eventually made Facebook so popular.

The Harvard version of Facebook was so instantly popular on campus that it overwhelmed Harvard's networks. No one could access the Internet until the problem was addressed due to the large amount of traffic the program garnered. Zuckerberg and his partners knew they were on to something. They ran the program out of his dorm room until 2004.

Designing the Solution

Later in 2004, they built Facebook to be used at other Ivy League universities, including Yale, Brown, Cornell, and Stanford. Zuckerberg left Harvard his sophomore year and moved the company to Palo Alto, California, to continue working with Facebook. He became the CEO.

Facebook was created with the user in mind. Users set up their own profile, where they could assign their own photo so that people could find them, list their interests and hobbies, and invite other friends to join their "friend" list. Blue and white were the primary colors. Some think this might have to do with Zuckerberg's red-green colorblindness; blue is easiest for him to see. Regardless, the design and concept attracted many people over the next decade, despite several layout changes.

Applying the Solution

Facebook had one million users by the end of 2004. Before long, Facebook was launched to other colleges and high schools nationwide and quickly grew in popularity. By December 2005, the site had more than 5.5 million users.

Until Facebook, the idea that a "social media" website could actually turn a profit did not exist. Although Zuckerberg initially fought the idea of selling ad space on the site, it wasn't until the site did so well that people realized there was money to be earned from such an idea.

So why was Facebook so successful, eventually beating out other platforms such as MySpace and Friendster? This is a hotly debated question. Some point to the fact that Facebook was much easier to use and navigate than other platforms, whereas others say it's due to its original hip, antiestablishment attitude.

The 2007 launch of the Facebook platform was definitely key to the site's success. The open **application program interface** (API) made it possible for third-party developers to create applications that worked within Facebook. Almost immediately after the API was released, it gained a massive amount of attention. Third-party programmers could create games and other add-ons that added to the already-popular Facebook.

The other key to Facebook's success was its "Like" button, which quickly began appearing all over the Internet and was used outside the bounds of Facebook. In fact, the term "like" has entered the national parlance. The Like button is a good example of the easy-to-use interface features that made Facebook friendly and appealing to the masses.

The Impact of the Solution on Society

Facebook's influence and mark on the world is an indelible and controversial one for sure. Initially seen as a boon to human and social connections—and certainly as a way to reconnect with old friends, classmates, and family living far away—it has been viewed by some as creating an artificially inflated sense of connection with others and the final death knell of online privacy. In a positive light, it helped make the world smaller, as people living many miles apart could connect and reengage in each other's lives in an immediate and consistent way. Facebook also changed the way people consume content. Facebook users are much more likely to check out news stories, sports scores, and videos posted by their friends than blind ads.

Some wonder if Facebook prevents us from communicating in the real world and making real connections with others. However, others, especially people living abroad, have relied on Facebook as a means to keep family and friends back at home connected to their lives, and vice versa.

Facebook also changed the way most people view privacy. With all the personal data posted and the algorithms that Facebook runs to cull our likes and dislikes, the definition of what is truly private has become a slippery slope. Some complain that the privacy settings

Zuckerberg's Personal and Philanthropic Life

The year 2012 was big for Zuckerberg. On May 18 of that year, Facebook went public. Its initial public offering (IPO) was for $16 billion, making it the biggest Internet IPO in history. On May 19—a day after Facebook went public—Zuckerberg and his longtime girlfriend, Priscilla Chan, were married. About one hundred people attended the surprise wedding at the couple's home. They thought they were there to celebrate Chan's graduation from medical school, but instead they witnessed Zuckerberg and Chan exchange vows. That same year, he also negotiated the company deal to buy Instagram.

Mark Zuckerberg and Priscilla Chan at their wedding in May 2012

Zuckerberg has used his millions to fund many philanthropic causes. Two noteworthy examples came in 2010. In September of that year, he donated $100 million to save the Newark public schools system in New Jersey. In December 2010, Zuckerberg signed the "Giving Pledge," whereby he promised to donate at least 50 percent of his wealth to charity over the course of his lifetime. Other Giving Pledge members include Bill Gates, Warren Buffett, and George Lucas. After his donation, Zuckerberg called on other young, wealthy entrepreneurs to join him in this pursuit.

have become so arcane that it's hard to know if users and their profiles are really protected from the greater Internet.

Regardless of the side one takes on these issues, Facebook proved that social networks could be profitable. Until Facebook, social media, in the sense it's used today, did not exist. It changed the online world, and these changes have proliferated throughout our world today.

Today, Zuckerberg and Facebook continue to do well, in spite of the controversy and criticism. *Time* magazine named him Person of the Year in 2010, and *Vanity Fair* placed him at the top of its "New Establishment" list. *Forbes* also ranked Zuckerberg at number 35 on its "400" list, estimating his net worth to be $6.9 billion. It is clear that Zuckerberg and his invention have made an indelible mark on technology and have changed the way people socialize, for better or for worse.

Timeline

1984
Mark Elliot Zuckerberg born in White Plains, New York

2002
Zuckerberg graduates Phillips Exeter Academy High School and attends Harvard College

2003
Facebook is launched by Zuckerberg and two colleagues from Zuckerberg's dorm

2004
Zuckerberg drops out of Harvard and moves the headquarters of Facebook to Palo Alto, California. By the end of 2004, Facebook has one million users

2005
Number of Facebook users tops 5.5 million

2010
Zuckerberg is voted *Time* magazine's Person of the Year

2012
Facebook goes public and makes Zuckerberg a billionaire

2012
Zuckerberg marries longtime girlfriend Priscilla Chan in Palo Alto

2013
Facebook makes the Fortune 500 list for the first time, and Zuckerberg becomes the youngest CEO on the list

Glossary

antivirus software A computer program that checks a computer or other device for viruses and then blocks them from harming or destroying it.

application program interface A set of tools and protocols for building applications.

BASIC A programming language that uses lists of simple English commands such as PRINT, INPUT, and GOTO.

cloud A term used to describe a main hub of storage on the Internet. All of your documents, files, photos, etc. can be saved to a cloud, which is accessible from many different devices.

code A set of instructions that tell a computer's screen how to operate.

compiler A computer program that translates from a different computer language into understandable symbols or the English language.

contemporaries People who are of the same generation or around the same age as each other.

data Information collected for analyzing.

debugging Ridding a computer of problems, called bugs.

domain The name or address of a website.

eccentric Different from what is typical; strange.

floppy disk A square-shaped device, made from plastic and metal, that was used to save and display files on early computers.

hacker Someone whose dogged determination and occasional flashes of inspiration permit him or her to solve difficult technical problems, perhaps at the detriment of another person or company.

hypertext Instructions written to tell the computer how text or a link should be displayed on a screen.

industrial design A type of architectural design usually associated with three-dimensional objects.

ledger A book that usually records movements of a company's funds.

Linux Foundation An organization set up to promote the Linux operating system and educate others about its benefit to the technological industry.

microprocessor Essentially, the computer's "brain"; what makes it function. All wires and other devices on the mechanism are placed together on a single integrated circuit.

monolithic principle The understanding that an entire electronic circuit could be made from one semiconductor material.

Nobel Prize A prize awarded every year to people who display exemplary achievement in literature, physics, chemistry, medicine, economics, or peace. It is named in honor of Alfred Nobel, a Swedish scientist.

open source Software that is available for anyone to download.

operating system The basic software that controls a computer's hardware and its applications.

patent A grant given by the government. It protects use of patented inventions in public.

philanthropist A person who gives away the money her or she makes to social or charitable causes.

quarantine To exclude a person or thing from society by physically keeping them or it in one location. This is usually a tactic done to keep sick patients away from healthy people, for a period of forty days.

semantic web An extension of the current web in which information is given well-defined meaning, better enabling computers and people to work in cooperation.

summa cum laude The highest honor awarded to a student upon graduation.

synchronization The process by which devices interact or respond in the same way at the same time.

transistor An electronic device that is used to increase or switch electronic signals and power.

viruses A harmful program that can corrupt a computer system and destroy data. A virus can also replicate itself.

wiki A website that allows visitors to make contributions, and change or delete its content in collaboration with other users.

Further Information

Introduction

Books

Essinger, James. *Ada's Algorithm: How Lord Byron's Daughter Ada Lovelace Launched the Digital Age*. Brooklyn: Melville House, 2014.

Frauenfelder, Mark. *The Computer: An Illustrated History from Its Origins to the Present Day*. London: Carlton Books, 2013.

Wei, James. *Great Inventions That Changed the World.* Hoboken, NJ: Wiley, 2012.

Websites

Computer History Museum
www.computerhistory.org

LiveScience: Computer History Timeline
www.livescience.com/20718-computer-history.html

Charles Babbage: Designer of Early Mechanical Computers

Books

Babbage, Charles. *The Writings of Charles Babbage.* Pearland, TX: Halcyon Press, 2009.

Ceruzzi, Paul. *Computing: A Concise History.* Cambridge, MA: MIT Press, 2012.

Dasgupta, Subrata. *It Began with Babbage: The Genesis of Computer Science.* New York: Oxford University Press, 2014.

Websites

Charles Babbage Institute
www.cbi.umn.edu/about/babbage.html

Plan 28
plan28.org

TEDxImperialCollege: The Greatest Machine That Never Was
www.youtube.com/watch?v=4rzAL5YwFow#t=164

Tim Berners-Lee: Inventor of the World Wide Web

Books

Alesso, H. Peter, and Craig F. Smith. *Thinking on the Web: Berners-Lee, Gödel, and Turing.* Hoboken, NJ: Wiley-Interscience, 2008.

Gifford, Clive, and Claudia Martin. *Tim Berners-Lee.* Inspirational Lives. London: Wayland, 2015.

McPherson, Stephanie Sammartino. *Tim Berners-Lee: Inventor of the World Wide Web.* USA Today Lifeline Biographies. Minneapolis, MN: Lerner Publishing, 2009.

Websites **TEDtalk: What Is the World Wide Web?**
ed.ted.com/lessons/what-is-the-world-wide-web-twila-camp

Tim Berners-Lee's Home Page
www.w3.org/People/Berners-Lee

Jeff Bezos: Founder of Amazon

Books Brandt, Richard L. *One Click: Jeff Bezos and the Rise of Amazon.com.* New York: Portfolio Trade, 2012.

Rossman, John. *The Amazon Way: 14 Leadership Principles Behind the World's Most Disruptive Company.* Seattle, WA: CreateSpace Independent Publishing Platform, 2014.

Stone, Brad. *The Everything Store: Jeff Bezos and the Age of Amazon.* New York: Back Bay Books, 2014.

Websites **Amazing Amazon Story**
www.youtube.com/watch?v=YlgkfOr_GLY

TEDtalk: Jeff Bezos at Princeton University
www.ted.com/talks/jeff_bezos_gifts_vs_choices

William Seward Burroughs: Inventor of the Modern Calculator

Books Campbell-Kelly, Martin, and William Aspray. *Computer: A History of the Information Machine. The Sloan Technology Series.* Boulder, CO: Westview Press, 2013.

Grier, David Alan. *When Computers Were Human.* Princeton, NJ: Princeton University Press, 2007.

Hardy, Lawrence H. *Another Ordinary Man: Computing and Networking History.* Seattle, WA: CreateSpace Independent Publishing Platform, 2012.

Websites **History of Computers and Computing**
history-computer.com/MechanicalCalculators/19thCentury/Burroughs.html

Further Information

How Stuff Works:
How William S. Burroughs Made It All Add Up
www.youtube.com/watch?v=X_rxERFpy-U

Alan Emtage: Inventor of the First Search Engine

Books

Halavais, Alexander. *Search Engine Society.* New York: Wiley & Sons, 2008.

Schmidt, Eric, and Jonathan Rosenberg. *How Google Works.* New York: Grand Central Publishing, 2014.

Websites

Alan Emtage's Website
www.alanemtage.com

Official Google Website
www.google.com

Douglas Engelbart: Inventor of the Computer Mouse

Books

Ceruzzi, Paul E. *Computing: A Concise History.* Cambridge, MA: MIT Press, 2012.

Isaacson, Walter. *The Innovators: How a Group of Hackers, Geniuses, and Geeks Created the Digital Revolution.* New York: Simon & Schuster, 2014.

Landau, Valerie, Eileen Clegg, and Douglas Engelbart. *The Engelbart Hypothesis: Dialogs with Douglas Engelbart.* Berkeley, CA: NextPress, 2009.

Websites

Bootstrap Institute
dougengelbart.org

Howstuffworks: How Computer Mice Work
computer.howstuffworks.com/mouse.htm

Bill Gates: Cofounder of Microsoft

Books

Manes, Stephen, and Paul Andrews. *Gates: How Microsoft's Mogul Reinvented an Industry and Made Himself the Richest Man in America.* New York: Cadwallader & Stern, 2013.

Wallace, James, and Jim Erickson. *Hard Drive: Bill Gates and the Making of the Microsoft Empire.* New York: HarperBusiness, 1993.

Websites **Official Microsoft Corporation Website**
www.microsoft.com

The Bill & Melinda Gates Foundation Website
www.gatesfoundation.org

Grace Murray Hopper: Inventor of the Computer Language Compiler

Books

Beyer, Kurt W. *Grace Hopper and the Invention of the Information Age.* Lemselson Center Studies in Invention and Innovation series. Cambridge, MA: MIT Press, 2012.

Coughlan, Michael. *Beginning COBOL for Programmers.* New York: Apress, 2014.

Misa, Thomas J., ed. *Gender Codes: Why Women Are Leaving Computing.* Hoboken, NJ: Wiley, 2010.

Websites **Grace Hopper Celebration of Women in Computing**
gracehopper.org

Grace Murray Hopper Award
awards.acm.org/hopper

Steve Jobs and Steve Wozniak: Inventors of the Apple I and Apple II Computers

Books

Isaacson, Walter. *Steve Jobs.* New York: Simon & Schuster, 2011.

Lashinsky, Adam. *Inside Apple: How America's Most Admired—and Secretive—Company Really Works.* London: Business Plus, 2013.

Wozniak, Steve. *iWoz: Computer Geek to Cult Icon: How I Invented the Personal Computer, Co-Founded Apple, and Had Fun Doing It.* New York: W.W. Norton & Company, 2007.

Websites **Apple, Inc.**
www.apple.com

Steve Wozniak
woz.org

Further Information

Jack Kilby and Robert Noyce: Inventors of the Integrated Circuit

Books

Kaplan, Fred. *1959: The Year Everything Changed.* Hoboken, NJ: Wiley, 2010.

Lécuyer, Christophe, David C. Brock, and Jay Last. *Makers of the Microchip: A Documentory History of Fairchild Semiconductor.* Cambridge, MA: MIT Press, 2010.

Malone, Michael S. *The Intel Trinity: How Robert Noyce, Gordon Moore, and Andy Grove Built the World's Most Important Company.* New York: HarperBuisiness, 2014.

Websites

Make Presents: The Integrated Circuit
www.youtube.com/watch?v=uSRIc-sEgPw

Nobel Prize in Physics 2000: Jack Kilby
nobelprize.org/physics/laureates/2000/kilby-autobio.html

John McAfee: Inventor of Antivirus Software

Books

Brown, Bruce C. *How to Stop E-Mail Spam, Spyware, Malware, Computer Viruses, and Hackers from Ruining Your Computer or Network.* Ocala, FL: Atlantic Publishing Group, 2009.

Ligh, Michael Hale, Andrew Case, and Jamie Levy. *The Art of Memory Forensics: Detecting Malware and Threats in Windows, Linux, and Mac Memory.* Indianapolis, IN: Wiley, 2014.

McAfee, John. *Computer Viruses, Worms, Data Diddlers, Killer Programs, and Other Threats to Your System.* New York: St. Martin's Press, 1989.

Websites

About McAfee, Inc.
www.mcafee.com

How Computer Viruses Work
www.howstuffworks.com/virus.htm

Pierre Omidyar: Inventor of eBay

Books

Draper, William H. *The Startup Game: Inside the Partnership Between Venture Capitalists and Entrepreneurs.* New York: Palgrave Macmillan Trade, 2012.

Gilbert, Sara. *Built for Success: The Story of eBay.* Makato, MN: Creative Paperbacks, 2012.

Woog, Adam. *Pierre Omidyar: Creator of eBay.* Innovators series. Farmington Hills, MI: Kidhaven Press, 2007.

Websites **eBay**
www.ebay.com

Omidyar Network
www.omidyar.com

James T. Russell: Inventor of the Compact Disc

Books Shelly, Gary B. *Discovering Computers: Student Success Guide.* Shelley Cashman series. Stamford, CT: Cengage Learning, 2012.

White, Ron, and Timothy Edward Downs. *How Computers Work, 10th ed.* Indianapolis, IN: Que Publishing, 2014.

Websites **"The Discoverer"**
web.reed.edu/reed_magazine/Nov2000/a_the_discoverer/index.html

How Stuff Works: James Russell and the Compact Disc
www.youtube.com/watch?v=PylWDGblkDk

Linus Torvalds: Inventor of the Linux Operating System

Books Cannon, Jason. *Linux for Beginners: An Introduction to the Linux Operating System and Command Line.* Seattle, WA: CreateSpace Independent Publishing Platform, 2014.

Morley, Deborah. *Understanding Computers in a Changing Society. 6th ed.* Stamford, CT: Cengage Learning, 2014.

Websites **Business Insider: Linus Torvalds Q&A**
www.businessinsider.com/linus-torvalds-qa-2014-6

Linux
www.linux.com

The Linux Foundation: Inside Linus Torvalds's Work Space
www.youtube.com/watch?v=HSgUPqygAww

Further Information

Jimmy Wales: Founder of Wikipedia

Books — Isaacson, Walter. *The Innovators: How a Group of Hackers, Geniuses, and Geeks Created the Digital Revolution.* New York: Simon & Schuster, 2014.

Meyer, Susan. *Jimmy Wales and Wikipedia.* New York: Rosen Publishing Group, 2012.

Websites — **Official Wikipedia Website**
www.wikipedia.org

TED Talk: The Birth of Wikipedia
www.ted.com/talks/jimmy_wales_on_the_birth_of_wikipedia

Mark Zuckerberg: Cofounder of Facebook

Books — Kirkpatrick, David. *The Facebook Effect: The Inside Story of the Company That Is Connecting the World.* New York: Simon & Schuster, 2010.

Mezrich, Ben. *The Accidental Billionaires: The Founding of Facebook: A Tale of Sex, Money, Genius and Betrayal.* New York: DoubleDay, 2009.

Websites — **Biography's Full Profile of Mark Zuckerberg**
www.biography.com/people/mark-zuckerberg-507402

Official Facebook Website
www.facebook.com

Index

Page numbers in **boldface** are illustrations. Entries in **boldface** are glossary terms.

Index